Introduction to international relations

MANCHESTER
UNIVERSITY PRESS

Introduction to international relations

Problems and perspectives

R. J. Barry Jones, Peter M. Jones
and Ken Dark

with Joel Peters

Manchester University Press
MANCHESTER AND NEW YORK

distributed exclusively in the USA by Palgrave

Published by Manchester University Press
Oxford Road, Manchester M13 9NR, UK
and Room 400, 175 Fifth Avenue, New York, NY 10010, USA
http://www.manchesteruniversitypress.co.uk

Distributed exclusively in the USA by
Palgrave, 175 Fifth Avenue, New York, NY 10010, USA

Distributed exclusively in Canada by
UBC Press, University of British Columbia, 2029 West Mall, Vancouver, BC, Canada V6T 1Z2

British Library Cataloguing-in-Publication Data
A catalogue record for this book is available from the British Library

Library of Congress Cataloging-in-Publication Data applied for

ISBN 0 7190 5252 1 *hardback*
ISBN 0 7190 5253 X *paperback*

First published 2001

10 09 08 07 06 05 04 03 02 01 10 9 8 7 6 5 4 3 2 1

Typeset in Stone fonts
by Koinonia, Manchester
Printed in Great Britain
by Bell & Bain Ltd, Glasgow

Contents

Preface

This book is intended as an introduction to international relations, with a difference. There are many excellent introductory texts in the field of international relations that offer a comprehensive overview of the subject at different levels of detail and sophistication. The purpose of this book, in contrast, is to provide a manageable review of a range of conditions, both historical and contemporary, and intellectual currents that highlight some of the more important changes in contemporary world affairs and continuing debates about its most effective study.

'Traditional' approaches to international relations have turned upon the central notion of the state. Three chapters in this book are devoted to a discussion of three 'levels of analysis' that lie within the 'traditional' approach. Through these three 'lenses' it is possible to see many of the central features of world affairs over the last three and half centuries and to gain a sense of how international relations have been studied for much of that time. The following three chapters then concentrate upon contemporary developments that may threaten the central role of the state in world affairs and explore their consequences for understanding and for academic study.

It is not the purpose of this book to delve deeply into many of the philosophical and methodological controversies that have beset the study of international relations within recent decades. Such controversies are important, but will mean little to students of international relations until they have secured some understanding of how the subject has been studied over the preceding centuries and some knowledge of the major developments that have taken place in the real world during that time. Moreover, as the chapter on 'fragmentation' (chapter 7) suggests, much of the intellectual turmoil within the academic study of international relations may, itself, be a function of the contemporary state of world affairs: the ending of the Cold War; the unusually dominant position of just one power, the United States of America; the pressures of globalisation; the growth of environmental problems; and the continuing intensification of a 'North–South' economic divide. The outer-reaches of 'critical' approaches are also, therefore, beyond the immediate concerns of this book. However, the influence of constructivist perspectives is to be found in respect of a number of the major issues and perspectives that are discussed.

Ethical questions are also beyond the purview of this book, critical though they are to a morally informed appreciation of developments in world affairs and central though they are to the formulation of acceptable and defensible international policy. However, the difficulties for democratic governance posed by the advance of globalisation and/or political fragmentation are considered directly and with some concern.

Overall, then, this study at the dawn of a new century seeks to offer the student a reasonably detailed introduction to a selection of the more important 'traditional' and contemporary approaches to the study of international relations and to those developments in international affairs, past and present, which these approaches reflect and, to an important extent, may have helped to sustain.

In its construction, this volume was also a genuinely collaborative effort. The neatness with which the various chapters were initially allocated to the different contributors did not, however, survive the process of detailed drafting and revision. The final versions of a number of chapters thus reflect the contributions of a number of the book's authors. However, the bulk of the authorship was as follows: chapter 1, the introduction, by Ken Dark with some contribution from Barry Jones; chapter 2, by Peter Jones with a significant input by Barry Jones; chapter 3 by Peter Jones, with a contribution by Barry Jones and advice from Charles Hauss; chapters 4, 5 and 6 by Barry Jones; chapter 7 by Barry Jones with assistance from Charles Hauss; and the brief conclusion by Barry Jones.

1 Perspectives on international relations

The world is changing rapidly. The patterns of contemporary change are complex and the consequences are far from clear. The ending of the Cold War raised hopes of a new era of peace and global harmony. The Gulf War to expel Iraq from Kuwait appeared to crystallise the 'New World Order'. However, such illusions were short lived. Brutal inter-communal conflict and genocide returned to Europe in the mayhem of the break up of the former Yugoslavia. The United Nations failed dramatically to restore domestic stability within Somalia and was forced into an ignominious retreat. The threat of major inter-state warfare might have receded for the foreseeable future, but conflict, death and destruction had clearly not been banished from the global scene.

International relations emerged as an academic field in the aftermath of the First World War. Its original purpose was to find political ways of avoiding war, or at least building a more stable and peaceful international order, and some hoped it would produce a cooperative and just world. Many international relations' scholars retain these high ideals, albeit tempered with a sense of bitter experience, although some adopt a more pessimistic outlook.

Almost from the start there was debate within the subject over how to achieve the goals which the discipline had set itself. Particular attention was focused on how to analyse world politics in order to discover the sources of change, conflict and war. Given the complexities of international affairs, it was essential that intellectual perspectives were developed that highlighted the most important features of an ever-changing reality.

The most appropriate conceptual framework of the discipline ('international relations theory') has thus remained the subject of controversy ever since that time, perhaps at no time more so than today. In this chapter some of the key debates in contemporary international relations theory, which affect other chapters of this book, will be outlined in an introductory manner.

Levels of analysis

This book, like most of international relations theory, investigates world politics in terms of three 'levels': individuals, states and systems.[1] These 'levels' are not the only possible categories which might be used, nor are they unproblematical in themselves, but each has been seen by some analysts as a basis for studying the subject.

Whether importance should be placed on states, individuals or systems forms the basis for a long-running debate in international relations theory: the so-called 'level of analysis debate'.[2] This is a somewhat confusing name, and can be questioned on two main grounds. First, it is unclear to what extent these levels are distinct in world political organisation. For example, they might alternatively be seen as intermeshed or co-existing, depending upon the definitions of the state or system which are used. Second, this debate was often about the 'unit' which should be used to study world politics, rather than the 'level' at which it should be studied. Moreover, there are other 'levels' which might usefully be discussed, such as the geographical extent and time scale (what is usually called the 'temporality') of analysis. If one is to pursue a 'level of analysis' debate there seems no reason to ignore these 'levels' as less relevant than those based on individuals, states or systems.

While it is conventional to think of the relationship between individuals, states and systems in terms of distinct levels, this tends to downplay the degree of interconnection necessary for each of the two supposedly higher 'levels' – states and systems – to exist. For example, states can be seen as comprised of individuals, or as either systems or part of systems. Likewise, international systems can be seen as comprised of states and individuals.

However, an emphasis on these three levels, individuals, states and systems continues to play an important role in discussions of every major issue in world politics. It is, therefore, important to begin by looking at the way in which focusing on each of these levels has led to specific approaches to this subject. However, here it will be argued that these are complementary, not exclusive or competing, aspects of international relations theory.

Individuals

An initial focus upon the individual provides a distinctive picture of world politics and the sources of international conduct. States, and the systems of states to which they give rise, can be seen ultimately as organisations, comprised of groups of people. These people have intentions, cultures, identities, values and beliefs which differ from time to time and place to place. Consequently states are neither single units, nor are they very similar to each other. Moreover, because they are not the only organisations comprised of individuals, focus on the individual suggests that the state may not be the only important unit of analysis.

If states are simply groups of individuals, it seems logical also to look at the potential role played by groups of people within states. Some of these may be formally encompassed within the government of the state, such as civil servants, soldiers or politicians, but some are not. These may comprise organisations, communities, social groups and movements. Examples include: firms, religious communities, groups within society (such as women) and social movements. 'Interest groups' may exist within a state, and might influence its policies. Such groups may develop agendas, identities and loyalties different to those promoted by the state government, but these agendas and interests too may conflict, leading to internal (intra-state) conflict or even civil war, as we have seen in Northern Ireland, Rwanda and Yugoslavia.

The patterns of loyalty and identity created by these means can be very complex. For example, an individual may simultaneously have identities and loyalties based on city or region, age, family, gender, nation, place of birth, political affiliation and religion. These 'multiple identities' are not always entirely the same as those promoted by the state within which that individuals lives, nor to those held by other inhabitants of the same state.

The boundaries of the state do not always limit these groups or organisations. Such actors may disregard state limits and yet comprise loyalties and identities much stronger than those to the state. Religious communities are, perhaps, the clearest example of this, where members of differing states might hold shared religious identities. These linkages may be strengthened by organisations existing for those holding specific loyalties, identities and beliefs. For example, in this case, a Church organisation may act across state frontiers, to serve its members around the globe.

Clearly, this type of 'transnational' relationship may lead to inhabitants of different states sharing loyalties, identities, beliefs and values in common. Moreover, it may lead to loyalties beyond and above those of the state. These relationships may also lead to stronger affiliations between members of different states than exist within those states themselves.

Of course, another type of relationship between individuals which creates transnational relationships is formed through economic activity. Economic exchanges may not involve shared identities and loyalties, but they too have the potential to create common interests, served by firms and other organisations, some of which operate within the state and some transnationally. An emphasis on the individual, therefore, suggests that more importance needs to be placed on the role of economic relationships and firms both within states, and transnationally. This is clearly illustrated in the role played by transnational corporations (TNCs) in creating transnational relationships and in acting as interest groups within states.

The political implications of this transnationalism are clear. If such exchanges, loyalties, identities and organisations operate transnationally, then they may act to promote specific policies or to prompt particular types of political activity. The transnational role of environmental conservationist groups is a very clear example of this. As discussed later, these groups may hope to persuade state governments to pursue specific policies which they support or propose, and may be organised on a world-wide basis. State governments may attempt to gain the support of these groups by favouring their interests above those of the state as a whole. If a state pursues policies opposing their agenda, this may become a source of intra-state conflict. Where some states support and others oppose such agendas, intra-state conflict of this sort can easily expand to include conflicts between – as well as within – states.

So, placing importance on the individual as a unit of analysis, emphasises the role not only of individuals, cultures, economics, gender, religion and so on, but of non-state groups and organisations as a whole. Whatever the precise consequences of their existence, these groups and organisations can be considered as potentially able to act in world politics. To put it another way, they are 'non-state actors' in international relations. Obviously, this also has implication for concepts (such as 'security') which in Realist terms would concern only the state. If the concept of security, for instance, is extended to cover individuals and non-state actors, its meaning changes dramatically.

Many analysts of world politics placing particular importance on the individuals, non-state actors and transnational relationships, would consider themselves 'Neo-liberals'. Since the 1980s, Neo-liberalism (exemplified by the work of Michael Doyle[3] and Mark Zacher[4]) has been the most widespread theoretical alternative to Realism in international relations. Some analysts see this contrast as so profound that they envisage the central debate about international relations theory in the 1980s and early 1990s as a theoretical controversy between Realists and Neo-liberals – the 'Neo-Realist:Neo-liberal debate'.

Today, most studies of world politics – whatever their theoretical basis – acknowledge that non-state factors have to be afforded some significance. Many Realists – such as Samuel Huntington and Richard Little, Barry Buzan and Charles Jones[5] – have encompassed some role for such factors in their theories. However, there is still controversy about how much importance should be placed on them and over what are their affects. But, here, all that it is necessary to recognise is that the very existence of these networks of non-state relationships based on individuals undermines still further the notion that it is simply relations between states which form the 'international system'.

States

Particular significance in politics and international relations has often been given to the existence and nature of the state. Indeed, the highly influential 'Realist' approach to international relations places the state at the centre of its analysis. Realism, of this sort, was so called because of the argument that, 'in reality, only relations amongst state governments 'mattered' in world politics. The governments of states acted in such a way as to create a single state viewpoint, which would be expressed in relations with other states and which would be identifiable by students of states' 'foreign policy'.

Such an approach to international relations underpinned classical 'Realism' within traditional perspectives, and viewed states as free, indeed obliged, to act in such a way as to pursue their interests. Classical Realism traces its origins to the pre-modern period, but in its twentieth-century form it is strongly associated with the work of Hans Morgenthau. Another, more moderate version, sometimes called 'The English School', is associated with scholars such as Hedley Bull and

Martin Wight. This 'school' still accepts the moral and practical priority of the state, and the society that it represents, but places much more importance on the historical development of world politics, and draws attention to the way in which states – while usually competing – can sometimes share values and establish rules of conduct. Consequently, these theorists argue, it is possible for an 'international society' to exist, which is similar in some (albeit rather weak) respects to other human societies with their rules and conventions.

The nature of states and, indeed, of the societies that they represent, is not, however, either as simple or uncontentious as often suggested within Realist approaches. States, as organisations, may be defined in many ways. Some definitions of the state emphasise the effective control of territory, others the existence of armies, or the ability to exercise centralised authority. Yet such definitions are of little help. Organisations others than states have had all of these characteristics, including the East India Company (an eighteenth-century forerunner of modern TNCs). Much more useful is the definition, first suggested by political anthropologists, that the state is defined by the existence of bureaucratic administration based on cities, over a polity (a political unit). Such a definition enables us to recognise states both as distinct from firms and transnational institutions, and from non-state political units.

Two main types of non-state polity have existed in global history: kin-based hunter-gatherer groups, and hierarchically organised 'chiefdoms'. The latter, exemplified by the polities of eighteenth-century Hawaii and seventh-century Ireland, shares with modern states territorial control, political centralisation and the waging of war. But chiefdoms lack the bureaucratic urban-based governments which characterise states. Defined in this way, there have been states for a very long time – since the middle of the fourth millennium BC, when the first states emerged in Mesopotamia (what is today Iraq and Iran). However, the 'modern state' or 'nation-state' is, as we have seen, a much more recent invention, dating from the seventeenth century and with its origin in the Treaty of Westphalia. It is important to recall that there have been other types of states, and other forms of polity, than the Westphalian state and that these were extremely enduring.

The abiding issue, however, is whether the modern state has, by its monopolisation of legitimate force, placed organised violence at the heart of its existence and functioning and, hence, presented the external world with an inherently violent face. Moreover, arguments that all states have served the interests of a few against those of the many, or that the character of some states have been seriously damaged by flaws in the cultural foundations of their societies, highlight further potential sources of aggressive international behaviour.

Systems

The 'highest' level of analysis in international relations focuses upon the character and consequences of the international system and/or the world system more widely conceived. Most analysts of world politics accept the concept of the 'international system'. However, the question of how to define international system has been one of the central problems of international relations theory. The possibility of defining such a system by reference only to states has already been mentioned, but there are several other possibilities. These depend both upon which units and types of relationship are believed to constitute a system of this sort, and on what is taken to define a 'system'.

Traditional concepts of the international system rested upon the centrality of the state. Viewing states as 'unitary actors', with a single set of intentions, allowed them to be treated as if they were individual members of a system – members with a single body (their territory) and a single mind (their government). Faced with an anarchical system – a system without a government to limit the actions of individual members – all states were conceived of as behaving in very similar ways. Each state would pursue its own interests, with no regard to higher moral principles, but as no two states had exactly the same interests all the time, these were sure to conflict. This conflict, in turn, would lead to competition between states, which might become war if violence seemed the only way for a state to achieve its goals.

Contemporary approaches to the international system, however, go further than the simple implications of international anarchy, to emphasise the way in technology, economics and the structure of the international system enhance and limit the possibilities open to states. Kenneth Waltz's 'Neo-Realism' sought to construct an analysis of the international system in terms of the structures which were, in turn, largely a function of the distribution of relevant capabilities amongst the members of the system.[6] A more recent version – 'Structural Realism' has sought to develop this further by accommodating a wide range of factors that underpin more complex patterns of structural differentiation that allow for states to occupy different positions within, for example, economic or politico-military structures.[7]

Realism, in its various forms, was popular during the Cold War with scholars and governments alike. But, since the collapse of the USSR, a great many analysts have come to regard Realism as a whole as intrinsically flawed, not least because this theory conspicuously provided no clues that the Cold War would end or the USSR collapse.

Beyond Realism

Recent developments in the analysis of complex human systems, further amplify more traditional approaches to the international system. Perspectives derived from mathematical 'complexity theory' vies states, and all other organisations, as themselves comprised of networks of inter-personal relationships. These can be seen as forming more limited networks within the wider pattern of non-state relationships, for example within communities, organisations and social groups. Yet, some or all of these relationships might intermesh, regardless of the formal boundaries of states, institutions and other groups. So, instead of having a single 'international system', one would envisage a wide array of 'complex systems' of this sort, some linked with and 'inside' each other. Rather than a cobweb, we might see the international system as a 'system of systems' – to some extent like a 'Russian doll' – in which one system can be 'opened up' to expose another.

Insights derived from complexity theory give renewed vigour to older views of world affairs not merely as relations amongst states but as networks of relationships between individuals and non-state groups. These networks could be seen as co-existing with relationships between states. Alternatively, inter-state relationships could be seen as relatively irrelevant compared to inter-personal relationships. In the opinion of John Burton,[8] whose work has already been introduced, the international system can then be seen as resembling a 'cobweb' of relationships between people, some of which had a formal political content (for example relationships between diplomats or civil servants) some of which did not. In this way, the international system might be envisaged not as a series of links between state governments, but as a global network.

Alternatively, a 'constructivist' approach may be adopted. According to this view, actors 'create' the international system simply through their own perceptions, beliefs, values and actions. They then proceed to act as if this system really existed.[9]

However, focusing on the individual does not necessitate either of these approaches. For example, although liberal institutionalists place much importance on the role of individual relationships in defining the international system, their approach to the international system tends also to emphasise institutions, interdependence[10] and the formation of international regimes.[11]

An 'institutionalist' definition of the international system emphasises the ways in which institutions bind together, and give unity to, the whole system. This perspective draws attention to the role played by institutions, such as the United Nations (UN), North Atlantic Treaty Organisation (NATO), the European Union (EU) and the Association of South East Asian Nations (ASEAN), in linking together states, regions and even the whole world into the system defined by membership of them. Defining the international system in the latter way is not as easy as it sounds, because there are some states which cannot or choose not to participate in international institutions, for example Switzerland (which is constitutionally strongly opposed to entering into alliances of any sort) is in none of the international institutions mentioned above.

Institutionalist views of the international system also hold out the prospect of regional or global 'governance'. By this it is meant that, while direct regional or global government may be impossible, there may be means of regulation and coordination which do not require this. Some institutionalists even argue that governance of this sort may eventually lead to regional or global government, perhaps through the development of organisations such as the EU, the North American Free Trade Area (NAFTA), the Group of Seven (G7) or the UN.

The concept of 'interdependence' has also been a very important part of the liberal institutionalist understanding of the international system . This concept may be defined broadly as consisting of patterns of mutual reliance between individuals, states or regions. For example, if the economy of one region requires oil produced in another, but that region depends upon the first for all its water supply, an 'interdependent' relationship exists. Interdependence might be seen to form and consolidate the international system, in that – once 'interdependent' in this way – participants cannot easily escape.

The exact definition and consequences of interdependence have been hotly debated by specialists in international politics, since the work of Robert Keohane and Joseph Nye in the 1970s.[12] In particular, the suggestion that the growth of 'complex interdependence' leads to fewer wars is still a subject of much controversy. This depends upon the view that when any two states become so interdependent any harm to one will also harm the other, then they will have too much to lose for it to be in either of their interests to fight.

Not all analysts of world politics would accept that interdependence exists at all, and many would claim that even if it could exist in theory it is impossible to demonstrate in practice. However, others claim that global interdependence is now so widespread that it affects every aspect of international politics, and is the basis for a single global political system resulting from 'globalisation'.

Another concept which has been widely used in liberal institutionalist theory as a means of discussing systems, is that of 'international regimes'.[13] A 'regime' in this sense is a common set of rules or conventions which are voluntarily entered into by two or more actors. These enable the coordination of action by different actors, despite their differing objectives. It has been argued for example, that global telecommunications and air traffic are governed by 'regimes' of this sort. Because regimes can exist as a situation without political dominance on the part of one actor, like international institutions they hold out the prospect of global 'governance' rather than global government.

It must be stressed that these differing approaches are not necessarily in conflict with each other. There are some scholars who would combine all, or almost any combination of, these different approaches to defining the international system. Indeed, a quite different definition of the international system can be based on economic relations. This 'materialist' definition assumes that flows of materials, services and resources are the basis for all international systems. Most analysts favouring this perspective draw on Marxist theory to interpret these flows as both intrinsically unequal and always based on exploitative relationships.[14]

Although originating in Marxist theories of world politics, by far the most widespread perspective today which defines systems in this way is 'world systems analysis'. This theory was introduced by Immanuel Wallerstein in the 1970s[15] and has been developed by scholars working in several disciplines, including international relations.

World systems analysis suggests that intrinsic economic inequality has given the international system a distinctive geographical form. Such a form comprises a 'core' (characterised by its technological and economic advantages) which exploits and dominates a 'periphery' (which is economically disadvantaged and in which lower levels of technology prevail). Each set of these relationships can be seen as two concentric circles, and each of these sets is termed a 'world system'. Because several sets of these relationships could co-exist, it is important to remember that many 'world systems' might exist at the same time.

There are, therefore, many competing definitions of the international system. Each emphasises some aspects of international relations as a means of defining the system, and downplays others. Each of these definitions carries with it a particular way of understanding international relations as a whole. Not all of these ways of studying the international system are, of course, wholly incompatible. Neither is simply combining them all possible, given the conflicting bases on which some are founded. Considering the international system in this way, therefore, highlights the central importance of theoretical discussion in the study of global politics. In this case, what we are studying depends upon which theoretical definition of the international system we adopt.

This discussion of the international system also shows the importance of which unit we choose as the basis of analysis. For instance, it has already been shown that if world politics is analysed using a state-centric approach the results will be different to if it is studied using an approach based on individuals. Likewise, if we adopt an approach which only concentrates on the international system (defined, say, in 'world systems' terms) then once again the result may differ. So, discussion of the definitions of and relationships between these levels and units of analysis is no trivial matter. It affects every aspect of how we study world politics, whether we are looking at the present or at the past.

However, we have seen that dividing international relations into these levels is primarily a matter of analytical utility. Each level cannot really be separated from the others in practice. So, while in this book we will attempt to integrate analysis on all three of these widely used 'levels' – individuals, states and systems – this is not to say that these are the only units of analysis, nor that they cannot be separated and studied independently. But international relations does not have a time limit. Nothing is 'too old' or 'too new' to fall outside this discipline. Nor is world politics ever entirely without change. So the analysis of change – even on a very long time scale – is central to the study of world politics.

Change

Change is both a very old and a very new issue in international relations. Although change was a key part of international relations during its early development as a discipline, during the Cold War few analysts of world politics paid much attention to this issue.[16]

However, the sudden (and largely unexpected) end of the Cold War, and the collapse of communism in eastern Europe and the former Soviet Union, highlighted the importance of understanding world political transformations. This has led to a rapid rise in the importance placed on the study of change in international relations, and an increasingly large number of studies of world political changes in the past and present. Today the analysis of change is at the heart of mainstream international relations, and theories of change are once again an important part of international relations theory as a whole.

Just as there are contrasting approaches to defining the international system, so too there are alternative views as to the sources and processes of global political change. To some extent these depend upon the degree of importance placed on individuals, states and systems as sources for and means of change. But they also depend upon two other important issues: the relative importance placed on time scales of analysis and on whether change is analysed in terms of events, processes or in some other way. So rapidly have theories of change proliferated that here it is only possible to outline a few, with reference to the individuals, states and systems division already described.

State-based views of change focus on the rise and decline of states and inter-state systems, as exemplified by the work of Robert Gilpin[17] and George Modelski[18] in international relations, and the related study by Paul Kennedy[19] in international history. All of these analysts draw attention to the relationship between the rise and fall of states and the rise and fall of inter-state systems. They stress the way in which, throughout modern history, particularly important states have been able to reshape the character of relations between themselves and other states to favour their own position.

In Gilpin and Modelski's opinions, these patterns of rise and decline have been so regular as to form 'cycles' ('long cycles' in Modelski's terminology) in world political history. Kennedy, Modelski and Gilpin have all argued that the rise and fall of states derives from the interplay of economic and political factors. Both Gilpin and Modelski have combined this view with an 'evolutionary' understanding of how change takes place. That is, economies, states and inter-state systems are supposed to 'co-evolve' through time, like biological organisms.

The part played by war in world political change is emphasised by both Gilpin and Modelski. Some international relations theorists see war as a cause of change – it plays this role in Modelski's theory – whereas others view war as an outcome of already ongoing changes. If war is seen as a result of change, then the successful management of change may be away of avoiding or even eliminating war.

Not all analysts favouring a state-centric view of world politics, prefer explanations of change based on economics, evolution, war or long cycles. Some Realist scholars place more importance on the role of system-level factors, external to individual states, in causing change. So, for example, in their study of long-term political change, Barry Buzan, Richard Little and Charles Jones[20] have drawn attention to properties which, they argue, structure the international system in particular ways. Changes to these properties affect system structure and lead states at specific periods in history to show distinctive types of behaviour.

Change can also be analysed using the individual as a unit of analysis. Attention may be given to the beliefs, values, perceptions and cultures of individuals as sources of political transformation. For example, some liberal institutionalist theorists have drawn attention to the way in which the emergence and decline of 'communities of knowledge' ('epistemic communities')[21] can cause world political change. Or the variety of the specifics of individual action can be highlighted, so that no common causes of change can be identified: each case much must taken separately and seen in its specific historical context.

A major theoretical issue facing all explanations of change based on individuals is how free the individual is to act. This point also applies to states or any other form of organisational actor in world politics. The critical question is to what extent contexts shape the ability to act ('agency'). These contexts, or 'structures' can be defined in terms of limiting or coordinating or regulating frameworks.

Consequently, the 'agent/structure' debate is essentially simply one about the degree to which actors are free to act! How this question is resolved, however, reflects upon the extent to which explanations of world political change can be framed in terms of individual intentions or actions.

Perhaps because of these problems, explanations based on individuals have been less widely used to study change in world politics than might initially be expected. Rather than basing theories on states or individuals, the most common way of explaining change in international relations is to look at systems-level dynamics.

How this systems-level analysis is conducted depends crucially upon the definition of the international system employed. For example, state-centric views may highlight the rise and fall of 'leading states' but 'world systems' explanations of change may emphasise the role of economic transformations. So, to understand world political changes in terms of systems, Realists seek state-based explanations while world systems analysts seek underlying economic patterns.

Analysts employing world systems perspectives have been especially active in the study of change. This activity has, however, been accompanied in the 1990s by an increasing diversity in 'world systems ' approaches. This has led to a series of debates which cut at the very heart of these perspectives. Such controversy surrounds the definition of world systems, with analysts suggesting that neither economics nor core–periphery relationships may be essential for world systems to exist. Another important debate centres on whether there have been many world systems in global political history, or only one. Proponents of the first view, notably Wallerstein himself, argue that the contemporary world system did not appear until about 1500.[22] Those who favour the alternative interpretation, suggest that there has been only one world system, originating in the Bronze Age Middle East. Consequently, this phase of theoretical vigour has been accompanied by intense questioning of the principal aspects of this theory by some of its leading exponents.[23]

Other scholars, examining change on a systems level, focus on the processes (or 'modes') of change rather than the causes. They examine how things change, rather than – or as well as – why they change. An excellent example of this approach, is Rosenau's concept of 'Turbulence'.[24] Basing his understanding of the international system on 'complexity theory', Rosenau draws attention to the similarity between the property of 'turbulence' in mathematics – a phase of intensified unpredictability and rapid change – and events in contemporary world politics. As such, Rosenau's perspective emphasises 'process' rather than events or specific causes.

Just as change can be seen in different ways by emphasising such aspects as events, processes, all of these levels can be analysed on a number of different time scales. Although most international relations theory has, in the past, concentrated on short-term changes, increasing attention is being given to long-term perspectives on world politics. This new interest in the long-term has been so pervasive in discussions of change that the study of 'change' and 'long-term change' have become almost synonymous in international relations theory.

There is, of course, some problem over how to define different time scales. One simple solution is to draw attention to the difference between short-term happenings, in the form of events, and 'structures' (for example, rules, organisations or values), which can outlast any individual event. In this way, 'short-term' and 'medium-term' time scales are created. But history shows that such structures seldom last without substantial change for more than a few centuries, so this does not allow for processes (such as urbanisation or industrialisation) which can operate over centuries or even millennia. So, another time scale – the 'long-term' – seems to be needed, on which such processes can be seen to operate.[25]

It is important, however, to remember that all long-term change is the outcome of short- (and medium-) term changes. But, short- and medium-term changes occur within long-term contexts also. Likewise, medium-term changes are comprised of short-term events, but also take place in a long-term context. So, in fact, just as discussions of events, structures and processes may all be essential to any such study, all these different time scales of analysis are inseparable in studying change in world politics.

Although this may seem an unavoidable conclusion, very few studies of change have tried to integrate these differing temporalities. However, the most recent international relations theory of change ('macrodynamics')[26] attempts to integrate all these temporalities and types of change into a single framework for analysis. This theory draws on a wide range of concepts from other fields in addition to new theoretical perspectives. It uses complexity theory to define and examine the dynamics of the international system, but employs approaches based on agency and structure to examine short- and medium-term political transformations. Envisaging human relations as networks of information flow, Macrodynamics highlights the role of information processing, information exchange and decision-making, alongside system dynamics (based on properties such as 'self-organisation'), to explain the dynamics of processes, structural transformations and events in world politics. It enables one to explain events in terms of unique circumstances, which are hard to predict, while analysing large-scale processes, which may operate on very long time-scales beyond the limits of every-day perception.

Macrodynamics has been used to study global political change through the span of human history, but has many implications for the world of today, and for the future. One such implication derives from the significance placed on communication. Macrodynamics suggests that the rate of change is closely connected to the rate of communication and information processing. The fast rate of information exchange and processing in the global system of the twenty-first century means, then, that 'history' is 'accelerating' in so far as change is occurring at a faster rate than previously.

Macrodynamics goes beyond this to suggest that problems arise as information flow exceeds the rate of information processing. If this occurs, the process of 'scalar stress' will operate, producing fragmentation, conflict and instability. If so, then only new types of information processing will avert serious political problems world wide, although the 'information revolution' already underway might be a sufficient innovation in information processing to avert disaster.

Alongside this theoretical diversity, perhaps the most striking aspect of the analysis of change in world politics is that its problems and questions are many of those which pervade the whole subject. However, important as they are, debates over the level of analysis, over agency and structure and about change are only some of the major concerns of international relations. By way of conclusion to this chapter, it is, then, worth simply mentioning a few of the other issues which this subject encompasses and which will be addressed later in this book.

Other core issues in international relations

It will already be clear that the name 'international relations' is something of a misnomer, because the subjects covered extend far beyond 'relations between nations'. In discussing other key areas of the discipline, not covered above, this misnomer may offer a beginning, by highlighting the significance of the relationships between states and nations. A states is not a nation, nor are most nations contained within a single state. This raises issues of nationalism and national identity, and those factors (including imperialism and decolonisation) affecting their expression. Nationalism and imperialism, in turn, bring to mind questions regarding war, revolution, conflict and – conversely – the possibility of international peace and cooperation. The reasons for, and elimination of, war has been an important focus of study within the discipline since its origins and still remains a central issue. Related topics within the broad church of international relations include: the nature and changing forms of war and security; the ethics and laws of war; and military technology and strategy.

Discussion of war, of course, immediately raises ethical issues. These, however, extend far beyond those which relate simply to fighting or conflict. International relations is concerned with issues such as the existence and enforcement of human rights, the validity of humanitarian aid and intervention, the ethics of economic practices and ethical issues relating to specific social groups, such as women. Another important area of ethical concern is the global environment and related themes, such as human population growth and migration.

The environment, population and migration are, however, all issues encompassed more generally within international relations. Environmental changes and impacts, the growth and health of the world's population and the movements of people are all issues of interest to the discipline. Environmental factors can also be aspects of security, either when they affect individuals, states or other actors or when the environment is at risk.

It will already be clear that it unwise to think about international relations using a narrow definition of what is 'political' or 'international'. International relations also includes the study of ideologies, identities, loyalties, beliefs, religions, perceptions, cultures and 'civilisations'. Likewise, the social contexts of actors can be seen as within its scope.

The way information is communicated, and materials and people can be transported are also important issues. For example, the global news media or the spread of literacy or computerisation are all issues of interest to scholars of international relations. Nor should the study of technology, be overlooked, as later discussed here in relation to globalisation.

Particular importance has also been paid to the relationship between politics and economics (international political economy), and especially to the ways in which political activity shapes economic behaviour. Consequently, not only are international trade and the distribution and mobilisation of resources of interest to international relations analysts, but issues of economic regulation and control. Likewise, importance might also placed on the institutions and firms taking part in the global economy, on business practices and on workers organisations. These are themes to which we shall return when discussing both globalisation and regionalisation.

All of these aspects are closely linked in relation to many specific issues, as will become clear from later chapters. Among these are debates about whether current global changes are producing increasing globalisation, a new tendency toward economic and political regionalisation or even world-wide fragmentation. Such debates, which illuminate many aspects of the subject of international relations, form the basic structure for the discussion of contemporary world affairs in this book.

Notes

1 For the classic expression of which see: K.N. Waltz, *Man, the State and War* (New York: Columbia University Press, 1959).

2 On which see: J. David Singer, 'The level-of-analysis problem in international relations', in K. Knorr and S. Verba, *The International System: Theoretical Essays* (Princeton, NJ: Princeton University Press, 1961), pp. 77–92.

3 Michael Doyle, 'Liberalism and world politics', *American Political Science Review*, 80 (1986): 1151–70.

4 Mark Zacher, *Governing Global Networks: International Regimes for Transport and Communication* (Cambridge: Cambridge University Press, 1996).

5 See: B. Buzan, C. Jones and R. Little, *The Logic of Anarchy: Neorealism to Structural Realism* (New York: Columbia University Press, 1993).

6 Kenneth Walt, *Theory of International Politics* (Reading, MA: Addison-Wesley, 1979).

7 See Buzan, Jones and Little, *The Logic of Anarchy*.

8 John W. Burton, *World Society* (Cambridge: Cambridge University Press, 1972).

9 On which, see: John Gerrard Ruggie, *Constructing the World Polity: Essays on International Institutionalization* (London: Routledge, 1998).

10 On which see: R.O. Keohane and J.S. Nye, *Power and Interdependence: World Politics in Transition* (Boston, MA: Little, Brown, 1977); and R.J. Barry Jones and P. Willetts (eds), *Interdependence on Trial: Studies in the Theory and Reality of Contemporary Interdependence* (London: Frances Pinter, 1984).

11 On which see: S. Krasner (ed.), *International Regimes* (Ithaca, NY: Cornell University Press, 1983).
12 Keohane and Nye, *Power and Interdependence.*
13 Krasner, *International Regimes*; and see also: V. Rittberger (ed.), *Regime Theory and International Relations* (Oxford: Oxford University Press, 1993); and the entry by Oran Young on 'Regime theory', in R.J. Barry Jones (ed.), *The Routledge Encyclopaedia of International Political Economy* (London: Routledge, 2001).
14 For a summary see: Chris Brown, 'Marxist approaches to international political economy', in R.J. Barry Jones (ed.), *The Worlds of Political Economy: Alternative Approaches to the Study of Contemporary Political Economy* (London: Pinter, 1988), pp. 122–41.
15 See, for instance, Immanuel Wallerstein, *The Capitalist World Economy* (Cambridge: Cambridge University Press, 1979).
16 Notable exceptions being: B. Buzan and R.J. Barry Jones, *Change and the Study of International Relations: The Evaded Dimension* (London: Pinter, 1981); and Robert Gilpin, *War and Change in International Relations* (New York: Cambridge University Press, 1981).
17 Gilpin, *War and Change.*
18 George Modelski, *Long Cycles in World Politics* (London: Macmillan, 1987).
19 Paul Kennedy, *The Rise and Decline of the Great Powers* (London: Fontana, 1989).
20 Buzan, Little and Jones, *The Logic of Anarchy.*
21 On which, see: Peter Haas (ed.), 'Knowledge, power and international policy coordination', Special edition of *International Organization*, 46 (1992): 1–390.
22 I. Wallerstein, *The Modern World System: Capitalist Agriculture and the Origins of the European World Economy in the Sixteenth Century* (New York: Academic Press, 1974).
23 See: A.G. Frank and B. Gills (eds), *The World System: Five Hundred Years or Five Thousand Years* (London: Routledge, 1993).
24 See: J.N. Rosenau, *Turbulence in World Politics: A Theory of Change and Continuity* (Hemel Hempstead: Harvester/Wheatsheaf, 1990).
25 On the varying time-scales see: F. Braudel, *On History* (London: Weidenfeld & Nicolson, 1980).
26 On which see: K.R. Dark, *The Waves of Times: Long-term change in International Relations* (London: Pinter, 1998), esp. chapter 4.

2 Individuals and groups in international relations

Patterns

Many of the problems of international relations have been attributed to the malign influence of bad, or misguided individuals, or to relatively small groups of evil, self-interested or deluded groups. Candidates for such ignominy are legion – from Ghengis Khan through to fanatical ideologues like Adolf Hitler. Cliques of greedy human beings, such as those associated with Cecil Rhodes during the violent exploitation of South Africa in the late nineteenth century, have also been seen as the sources of many past international and inter-societal conflicts. Finally, the failings of both individuals and policy-making groups as effective decision-makers have also been blamed for much of the violent conflict that has besmirched the modern era. The widespread policy-making 'blunders' that contributed to the outbreak of the First World War in 1914 are one of the most prominent group of failures of collective decision-making to attract the attention of historians and international relations' analysts.

If many of the greatest ills of modern international relations have been attributed to individuals and small groups, so too have many of the achievements and advances. The formation of the League of Nations owed much to the idealism of Woodrow Wilson, the President of the United States of America during the First World War. Much of the joint resolve of Great Britain and the United States of America during the Second World War has been linked to the personal influence of Prime Minister Winston Churchill and President Franklin Delano Roosevelt. Equally, many analyses attribute the successful handling of the Cuban missile crisis to the judicious policy-making of President John F. Kennedy's group of crisis decision-makers – excom.

Certainly, many of the most dramatic developments in international relations throw a sharp light upon leading decision-makers.

Government leaders, military commanders and members of high-level advisory groups, all come under intense scrutiny during periods of international tension and/or major developments in international relations, such as peace conferences or the negotiation of new international institutions. Moreover, there is also a marked tendency for dramatic international developments to concentrate power and influence in the hands of leading members of governments as the need for rapid and decisive decision-making grows: a tendency most evident in the case of the mature democracies – Great Britain and the United States of America – and the marked level of state leadership developed in such times of major threat as the Second World War. Finally, some political leaders, or would-be leaders, have sometimes sought to generate international tensions as a way of attracting attention and/or of securing a concentration of power and influence in their hands, as demonstrated by the behaviour of Slobodan Milosevic in the numerous conflicts that sundered the former Yugoslavia during the latter 1990s.

'Domestic' sources of international behaviour

- Great (or bad) men and women
- Policy-making systems
- Political institutions and cultural systems
- Interest/pressure groups
- Geo-political conditions (including economic systems and resources)

Great (and/or bad) men and women

In the past, history was generally written as the history of the influence of great individuals, whose purposes directed their states and societies and whose successes, or failures, determined the long-term developments. Modern historiography – the theory and practice of research and writing in history – has often ascribed greater influence to wider political, social and/or economic forces in the shaping of the fate of humanity. International relations, however, often refocuses attention upon the role and influence of individuals, acting as individuals or as members of central decision-making groups. The course and outcome of the Second World War highlight such issues ideally, in the continuing debates about the level of responsibility assigned to Adolf Hitler for the outbreak of the war and the scale and depth of the defeat ultimately imposed upon Nazi Germany. The character and role of Winston Churchill is equally central to the persistent questions about the possibility that Great Britain might have made peace with Germany after the major defeats of May 1940, and, by not doing so, aided rather than resisted the aggressive expansion of Nazism. Such debates remain controversial and largely unresolved because of the complexity of the circumstances under which individuals appear to be able to exercise major influence, and the significant lack of precise comparability between any two cases of such apparent influence.

If the course of history has often been attributed to the influence of 'great' men and women, so too has much of the history of human conflict been attributed to the malign influence of 'bad' men and women (mainly men). In pre-modern times, the mobilisation of substantial military forces, and their effective deployment in armed conflicts, rested to a considerable extent upon what Max Weber termed the *charismatic* qualities of leaders and their closest associates.[1] Such charisma was often reinforced, or even conditioned by religious doctrines and/or principles of inherited political position and power. However, individuals or small groups with the ambition for conquest and the practical ability to mobilise armed forces of sufficient size and quality, were the necessary ingredient for the outbreak of international or inter-societal conflicts of any scale, as the Viking incursions into the increasingly stable societies of Western Europe at the start of the second millennium demonstrated.

The consolidation of the modern state and the modern inter-state system was, in large part, the story of the gradual conversion of charismatic power into more routinised forms of power and influence by the rulers over the ruled. The personal ambitions of individuals and groups could now be pursued through a two-step process: first, the achievement of a position of power and influence within the state apparatus; and, second, the use of state power to achieve more personal aims and objectives. However, the consolidation of the state, its institutions and personnel, often qualified the extent to which purely personal ambitions, to the neglect of all other considerations, could be pursued by those achieving prominent positions within the state structure, if only because of the potential damage that such behaviour could inflict upon the institutions of the state itself.

Well-formed states within economically prosperous societies have thus exerted a moderating influence upon the pursuit of personal purposes by individuals and groups. However, such restraints are by no means consistent, constant or universal. Other kinds of states offer different individuals and groups varying sets of opportunities and constraints, even when those states are nominally democratic. Thus the influence that can be exerted directly by wealthy groups is far higher within the electoral and political system of the United States than it is in most Western European democracies.

Changing circumstances may also alter the patterns of constraints and opportunities facing individuals and groups. Political instability and/or economic collapse may both undermine the solidarity of the state and its institutions and permit greater than normal influence by individuals or groups – as witnessed by the influence exerted by Lenin's Bolsheviks in revolutionary Russia or Adolf Hitler's Nazi party in the depression-hit Germany of the early 1930s.

Confrontation by major external threat may also reduce the constraints facing individuals or groups within well-established states, and even democracies. The effective power and influence of the leaders of British governments during the two world wars was remarkable within such a highly institutionalised parliamentary democracy. However, the constraints that persisted within the British system remained far higher than within a totalitarian system like Nazi Germany, as the ejection from office of Britain's first Second World War Prime Minister – Neville Chamberlain – after an unfavourable debate and vote within the House of Commons demonstrated dramatically.

Interest groups

The malign influence of groups of self-interested people has long been part of the demonology of international relations. Attempts to identify economic interests as the well-spring of international behaviour, in general, and of international aggressiveness, in particular, are common to a wide range of students of international relations, from some of the simpler versions of Marxism to critical liberals.

The core of interest group interpretations of international conduct rests upon two propositions: first, that cohesive interest groups will seek to maximise their advantages through politics and the international conduct of the states within which they reside; and, second, that interest groups with greater capacities for influence over the political system will prove more successful than less influential groups in securing such advantages.[2] Such propositions are inherently plausible, apparently supported by much anecdotal evidence, but often quite difficult to test in a systematic manner.

The acceleration of mercantile imperialism from the seventeenth century onwards has often been attributed to the growing prominence of groups of traders within the economic and political systems of a number of pivotal Northern European societies and their gradual displacement of feudal influences. The high (or low) point of such influences was then witnessed in the activities of imperial adventurers like Cecil Rhodes, and his commercial allies within influential British circles, in starting such late nineteenth-century wars of imperial conquest as the Matabele Wars in what is now Zimbabwe and the Boer war against the Afrikaner republics in South Africa. The pernicious influence of major arms traders upon the outbreak of international conflict has also often been the subject for considerable speculation.

Policy-making groups

Apart from the influence of interest groups upon the policy-making process of states and societies, it is also the case that international policy-making in most mature and complex societies is an essentially collective process. Final decisions are often made by groups, albeit relatively small, of senior members of governments and their advisors. Moreover, the wider governmental system is also involved critically in the policy-making process as a source of essential information and advice about policy issues and as the means through which the majority of policy decisions are actually implemented in practice.

Many accounts of the outbreak of the First World War in 1914 thus emphasise the nature and role of the groups of leading policy-makers within the major participating states, the policy-making systems within which they operated and, in particular, the military planning and advice with which decision-makers were presented and, to a considerable extent, constrained as they contemplated the decisions that led ultimately to war.[3]

The catastrophic decision-making that precipitated the First World War is frequently contrasted with the highly 'successful' policy-making undertaken by President J.F. Kennedy's administration during the Cuban Missile Crisis of October, 1962. Here, success has been attributed to the determination of a group of singularly effective decision-makers to keep policy-making 'rational' and well deliberated under the greatest of pressures. The critical decision-making group –

the executive committee (excom) – was both well constituted and well managed according to such laudatory and optimistic interpretations.[4]

The policy-making of successive US administrations has not, however, always been seen in such a favourable light as that of the Cuban Missile Crisis decision-makers. The progressive involvement of the United States in the Vietnam War was a case of longer-term policy-making that was rarely confronted by a situation as acute – in terms of threat and time constraints – as the Cuban Missile Crisis – and was therefore able to evolve step-by-step, or incrementally, and to drift onwards along what many came to believe was a disastrous course.[5] In the case of the Vietnam War, central decision-making groups and the wider policy-making system were both involved in the process of progressive commitment and its justification in the face of apparent lack of practical success and growing disquiet amongst the American public.

Such is the potential influence of central individuals and decision-making groups that much of human history has thus been written in terms of the influence and roles of 'great men' and the explanation of many serious human conflicts couched in terms of malign or misled individuals and groups. The problem of such an approach to international developments is, as will be apparent from much of the subsequent discussion, that it is often very difficult to distinguish the role of any individual or group of policy-makers from the influence of the wider international system that bears upon their decisions, or, more particularly, the society within which they have been socialised and by which they continue to be influenced and/or constrained. Equally problematic is the role of the intellectual and contextual constraints under which all human beings necessarily have to act and which may all too easily undermine the effectiveness and appropriateness of the decisions that they make under conditions of stress, shortage of time and considerable uncertainty.

Sources

The focus in this section will be upon the problems faced by individuals, groups and governmental systems, in making effective decisions about international conduct, rather than upon the wider political and societal influences that shape the broad context within which such policy-makers operate. These wider influences are considered more fully elsewhere in this book, primarily in chapter 3.

Individuals as constrained decision-makers

Many of the difficulties witnessed in international relations and the conduct of individual states (or, indeed, other actors upon the global stage) stem from the constraints under which they have to operate as decision-makers. It is often hoped that such decision-makers will operate 'rationally', but the problems of being wholly rational, by any precise meaning of that term, remain insurmountable.

Forms or modes of rationality in international politics

- Rational action at the state level (what action will best serve the well-being of a state given the prevailing international situation and the state's position within it)
- The rationality of organisations, departments and their members (what will suit an organisation/department in terms of policy influence and/or the acquisition of valuable resources)
- The rationality of influence-seeking individuals and groups (what will suit personal interests in the pursuit of influence and power)

There are many definitions, criteria and levels of rationality. Some focus upon the patterns of activity that a state, or any other actor, actually undertakes within the environment in which it has to operate. Thus a state might be deemed to have acted rationally if it decides to defend itself militarily if it is subject to an armed attack by some other state. Such a conception of rationality assesses each actor, and its behaviour, by the criteria of some model of *rational action*.[6]

Such rational actor models of state (or human) conduct, are, however, open to some serious objections. To produce any neat specification of the action that a rational actor ought to undertake within any situation requires two significant analytical steps. First, the range of values and purposes that the actor has to consider has to be simplified and reduced: if a potentially infinite range of values and purposes could be pertinent to an actor's course of action then it may be impossible to determine what course of action the actor should select or to calculate what the actor is likely to select in practice without prior knowledge of the preferences of that particular actor, and this would, in turn, destroy the general applicability of the rational actor model being employed. Second, the situation facing the actor will also have to be simplified analytically: a situation of potentially infinite complexity will prevent any clear and stable prediction of the course of action that the actor should, or will, select. Thus, nuclear strategic doctrine has conventionally been analyzed in terms of rational action models that prioritise the value of avoiding defeat at the expense of the alternative priority of minimising loss of life and damage to property: a preference which is not, and does not have to be, shared by all.

Problems with rational actor models have encouraged the adoption of an alternative approach to rationality in the making of policy. Criteria have been developed for a *rational decision-making process*. This approach makes no direct judgements about the quality of an action selected by any actor, but focuses, in contrast, upon the manner of making that selection. It thus concentrates upon processes rather than upon outcomes.

Influential students of decision-making, including Herbert Simon[7] and Charles Lindblom,[8] have established the criteria of rational decision-making:

- The first, and most obvious, criterion of rational decision-making is that the need (or occasion) for a decision is properly recognised: if an important development in the policy environment is simply missed, it is likely that inappropriate actions will result.
- The second criterion of rational decision-making is that comprehensive information about the situation requiring a decision is acquired and processed fully by the decision-making body: if any item(s) of information is (are) missed it is possible that the view of the situation will be erroneous and an inappropriate course of action selected.
- The third criterion of rational decision-making is that those values, objectives and purposes of the decision-makers (and their society) that may be affected by the new situation are identified and ranked in order of priority: if the situation has implications for values that are not recognised, or properly ranked, by the decision-making group, then the course of action ultimately selected may not be one that actually serves the needs or interests of the group, and of the broader society as well as some alternative course of action.
- The fourth criterion of rational decision-making is that all possible courses of action that might be selected within the new situation are identified and displayed: any neglected possible course of action might have been the course of action that would

have best served the needs or interests of the group and its society.

- The fifth criterion of rational decision-making is that the implications for the ranked set of values and objectives of each possible course of action is computed in the light of the prevailing situation and the comprehensive information that has been accumulated: unless exhaustive and effective calculations of the consequences of all possible courses of action have been undertaken, it will be impossible to ensure that the best course of action will be selected.
- The sixth, and final, criterion of rational decision-making is that the course of action that will ensure the maximum benefit for the values and objectives of the group and its society, as determined by the previous process of comprehensive evaluation, is actually selected.

Formal criteria of rational decision-making

- Correct identification of a development requiring a decision
- Acquisition of comprehensive information about the development
- Identification and ranking of all values affected by the development
- Identifiation of all possible courses of action that can be taken
- Calculation of the implications for the ranked set of values of all the possible courses of action
- Selection of that course of action that produces the highest level of benefit for the largest number of the most highly ranked values

Satisfying all the criteria of rational decision-making is impossible for human beings when dealing with complex and dynamic international situations, as will be seen later in this chapter. The problems of meeting such criteria have encouraged greater interest in the processes of decision-making that individuals and groups actually adopt when confronting complex policy problems. Such a focus, in turn, directs analytical attention towards the processes of perception and cognition at the level of the individual human being and to the processes of group decision-making at the level of collective policy-making.

The sheer complexity of the environment with which the individual person has to cope means that selectivity is essential when the individual interacts with that environment. From the potentially overwhelming mass of information being transmitted by the senses, primarily of sight, hearing and smell, the individual selects the information that is of greatest significance. Significance is, in turn, determined by the ideas that the individual has already developed about the surrounding world – how it functions, what features are of the greatest importance – and which have been acquired by past education and experience. The set of general ideas about the nature and importance of various features of the surrounding world form the cognitive structure and the belief system of the individual. The cognitive structure and belief system of the individual, in turn, govern the perceptual filters that the individual applies (usually unconsciously) to the flow of incoming data from the surrounding world.

The problem with the cognitive structures and belief systems of individuals is that, while they are essential to orderly interaction with the physical and social environment, they also impose potential constraints upon the ability to the individual to accept, or interpret effectively, information about that environment which may not fit neatly with existing ideas or beliefs. Such resistance to novel or challenging information may not be merely passive. The work of Leon Festinger, in his theory of cognitive dissonance,[9] has highlighted the way in which the human intellect may act positively to try to avoid uncomfortable intellectual and personal challenges by blocking the receipt of challenging information or by counteracting its effects. Through such techniques as evasion or denial, of reversing the logical implications of new information, or of searching for information that is supportive of established ideas, an individual can resist challenging information until it becomes effectively irresistible, at which point a rapid and dramatic reversal of opinion may take place.

Much of the force of resistance to challenging information or experience comes from the way in which individual ideas or values are tied in with other important ideas or central values. It is not, therefore, merely a matter of changing one idea or value, but of prompting a set of inter-related adjustments of ideas and/or values. Resistance to such cumulative change is likely to be more determined than would be resistance to one, isolated idea or value.

Human beings are also limited in their computational capabilities. Few, if any, individuals can anticipate all the consequences of a wide range of possible courses of actions. Not only would such comprehensive computation require formidable intellectual capabilities, but it would also be highly time consuming. In the effort to limit the time and effort involved in reaching important decisions, individuals thus have a tendency to limit serious consideration to a relatively small number of possible courses of action, to select the first option that appears to be relatively satisfactory in terms of the prevailing situation and to alter the course of action only when compelled to do so by subsequent developments and then to the minimum extent necessary: such patterns of decision-making have been termed *satisficing* behaviour with the *incremental* development of policy.

The implication of the constraints created by the cognitive and perceptual mechanisms with which human beings operate is that the rationality (or internal logic) of the decision-making is fundamentally subjective rather than objective. Most human decisions thus flow from the limited number of values considered by an individual or by groups, from the limited information acquired and considered, and from the relatively brief review of the strictly limited number of possible courses of action actually considered. Some rationality is maintained through the consistency that is sustained within this process, but this is not rationality by the more ambitious criteria of rational action or rational decision-making.

The limited 'rationality' of practical decision-making

- Decision-making starts from the basis of current policies
- Decision-makers seek to maintain existing policies as far as possible
- Decision-makers attempt to adapt exisiting policies in the face of new developments and to minimise change
- Wholly new policies will be devised only if all attempts to adapt existing policies have clearly (and often dramatically) failed

Groups as imperfect policy-makers

Policy-making by groups or complex organisations offers some means of compensating for the limitations suffered by individual decision-makers, but also contributes its own, distinctive difficulties. Groups and complex organisations embrace far more accumulated knowledge and understandings than are available to most individuals. They also provide an opportunity for a wide range of ideas and arguments to be directed towards any policy-making problem. Diversity of information and views may thus contribute to the richness, and ultimately the effectiveness, of the processes of deliberation and decision-making, with regard to complex policy questions.

A wide range of historical and anecdotal evidence, however, also revealed the down-side of group and organisational policy-making. Within smallish groups, the major difficulty is the development of *group-think*:, a common view amongst the members of the group that is reinforced by a powerful array of intra-group social-psychological processes and which can become highly resistant to challenge or change.[10] Such group-think may be particularly dangerous when it emerges within senior governmental policy-making groups at times of major international crises, such as Britain's Suez Crisis in 1956, or within the longer-term development of policy for serious, and hazardous, issues, such as the involvement of the USA in Vietnam in the 1960s.

The stresses that characterise serious policy-making, and that intensify at times of international crises, also influence the quality of decision-making. Up to a certain level, stress sharpens thinking and impels concentration upon the task in hand. Policy options may be thought through more thoroughly and routine obstacles to effective deliberation and decision-making within the wider policy-making system may be overcome. Unfortunately, intense and sustained stress can become unmanageable, inducing sub-optimal task performance and ultimately pathological responses amongst those affected. Tendencies towards group-think may certainly be reinforced by protracted experience of stressful situations, as initial uncertainties give way to excessive confidence in selected policy choices.

Group-think may develop at any point within a complex, governmental system. Also the system itself could contain its own problems which work against effective policy-making. The component parts of a complex governmental system often develop a life of their own. Specific sub-cultures may be developed within different departments or sections of the system and these may exert a profound influence upon the content and quality of policy advice coming from those departments, affect their ability to coordinate effectively with other departments, and, ultimately, have an effect upon the way in which they implement policy decisions made by higher authorities within the system.

Many studies of policy-making in complex organisations have identified the ways in which specific departments and sections develop distinctive views of the general policy problems faced and seek to promote particular interests within the wider policy-making process. Members of such departments and sections are progressively socialised into the 'departmental views' and have to demonstrate

Decision-making in groups

Advantages

- Wider range of knowledge brought to bear
- Wider range of ideas, interpretations and proposals
- Options can be thoroughly discussed and debated

Disadvantages

- Pressures towards conformity and the exclusion of mavericks
- Mutual reinforcemnt of policy preferences and confidence in inappropriate policies, 'Group Think'

adherence to them if they wish to move up the internal promotions' ladder. Such departments and sections also develop routinised ways of undertaking their various tasks: standard operating procedures that also condition what they think is feasible and that constrain the way in which they undertake assigned tasks. The diversity of 'departmental views' and varying standard operating procedures reinforce tendencies towards fragmentation within governmental policy-making systems and can lead to the kind of confusion that characterised the contradictory policies of the US State Department and the Central Intelligence Agency towards the South Vietnamese regime of President Diem at the time of its overthrow in 1963.[11]

Sustained high levels of stress will, moreover, contribute to a general reduction in the efficiency of policy-making and increased rigidity. Cumulative fatigue and sustained stress combine together to undermine the vitality and confidence of policy-makers at all levels and expose the system to the growing danger of failures of information gathering and assessment, inadequate policy calculations and, thence, inappropriate policy-decisions. [12]

Solutions and problems

There has been no shortage of solutions proposed for the many problems faced by individuals, groups and governmental policy-making systems as they face up to complex and potentially costly decisions on their international conduct. The difficulty with many such solutions, however, is that they usually encounter all but intractable practical problems and may even require profound changes to international and national political systems.

Better individual decision-makers

Eliminating the malign influence and disastrous effects of dangerous individuals has often seemed to be one of the most promising paths to the elimination, or at least substantial reduction, of international conflict. Psychologists, social psychologists and sociologists have proposed personality tests to establish the suitability of individuals for high political office. Such tests, however, often prove to be an imperfect guide to behaviour prior to pathological tendencies actually being exhibited by those who have achieved positions of power and influence.

Psychological factors also affect policy-making by non-pathological individuals, as has been seen. Personality tests have, again, been suggested as a means of eliminating from the selection process those who might be unacceptably prone to excessively rigid thinking and decision-making, or who are unduly vulnerable to the kinds of social-psychological pressures that lead to group-think. More seriously, however, the proposal of personality tests alone does nothing to alter political systems in such a way as to prevent the election of unsuitable leaders in democratic systems or the seizure of power by flawed personalities in non-democratic polities.

There are two primary difficulties with such proposals of psychological profiling, to rule out potential psychopaths and to select in favour of those equipped for effective decision-making. First, there are real difficulties in differentiating in advance between those 'conviction politicians', who are clear and determined in their commitment to political principles that may be currently unfashionable, and psychopaths who will plunge themselves and everyone else into disaster in the pursuit of fanciful, if not fatal, political goals; Winston Churchill's obdurate opposition to the appeasement of Nazi Germany in the years immediately before the Second World War being an excellent example of this difficulty. It is equally difficult to differentiate those whose confidence and firmness will enable them to maintain policy commitments through difficult times from those who will lapse into a damaging condition of group-think.

The second, no less serious, difficulty with the advocacy of personality tests for potential leaders, is their failure to address the changes in political systems that would be necessary for such tests to have a decisive influence upon the selection of senior political leaders and government members. Dictatorships are unlikely candidates for reforms aimed at the selection of reasonable and flexible political leaders. Democracies, too, have traditionally been based upon the principle that qualification for election to office should be as little constrained as possible and that electors should enjoy as wide as possible a choice of those for whom to vote. Limiting candidates to those conforming to relatively narrow psychological criteria might make the world a slightly safer place but it might look distinctly undemocratic to contemporary eyes.

More rational actions

The many, spectacular upheavals that have afflicted international relations in the past have also prompted proposals for more rational decision-making by individuals and groups of policy-makers. Some of the major 'debates' within the study of international relations have also been arguments about the types of rational action models that policy-makers ought to adopt in their conduct of international relations. Political Realists have thus traditionally advocated a model of rational action that emphasises the central requirement of maintaining, or enhancing, the capacity of the state to exert effective influence over other states within which it interacts, at all times and under all circumstances. Such an imperative, it is argued, flows from the uncertain and dangerous nature of the international system and the consequential folly of neglecting the need to sustain the 'power' of the state as a means of meeting any challenges that the system might reveal.

Political Idealists have challenged such a pessimistic vision of international relations and advocated, in contrast, a model of rational action for policy-makers that encompasses a wider set of human interests and concerns than those of the Realists, and that also makes different, and possibly more optimistic, assumptions about the sources of conduct in human, political and international affairs. They thus contend that action based upon an assumption that international conditions can be significantly improved is both appropriate and rational, given the wider set of real human needs and interests served by behaviour that generates improved conditions.

As E.H. Carr demonstrated in his classic book *The Twenty Years' Crisis*, however, unqualified Idealism can lead countries into acute danger when other states embark upon threatening courses of international action.[13] Carr also argued, however, that unqualified Realism can also lead policy-makers into a form of misanthropic pragmatism, in which assumptions that the worst may happen can all too easily precipitate developments that ensure that the worst will happen. Carr's call for a judicious combination of Realism and Idealism indicates, in effect, the difficulties and dangers of trying to base international conduct on any one, necessarily simplistic model of rational action in international affairs.

More rational decision-making

The difficulties confronting the adoption of rational action models has encouraged attention to turn to improvements in the processes of decision-making. Rational decision-making processes appeared to offer one promising path to a better international future. Some of the intellectual constraints upon rational decision-making have been indicated in the earlier discussion, however. There is also a set of irreducible practical and logical obstacles to satisfying the criteria of rational decision-making.

TIME AND EFFORT

The problem with the standard criteria of rational decision-making is that they make no reference to time or effort. Foreign policy decision-making takes place in real time and involves real human effort. Time is a compelling constraint because the situation that warrants a decision may encompass deadlines. Unlimited time cannot therefore be spent upon the activities of information acquisition and processing, value identification and ranking, the display of policy options, and the calculation of policy consequences, because critical deadlines may be past before these processes are complete. The pressures of time upon decisions may thus render it irrational to try and satisfy all the criteria of fully rational decision-making.

The expenditure of effort illustrates a further paradox of rationality within decision-making in a complex environment such as the international system. Effort has to be expended across time, so the time constraint upon rational decision-making process will again apply. The benefits of further expenditures of effort will also begin to decline at some stage in the decision-making process. Indeed, it is likely, that the effort required to acquire an additional item of information might rise rapidly as increasing levels of information have already been secured, while the value of that additional information might be declining. When the marginal value of additional information falls below the marginal cost of acquiring that information, it would be irrational, in one sense of the term, to continue to expend effort to acquire additional information.

DYNAMIC UNCERTAINTY

The discussion of improving decision-making processes thus far has been based, implicitly, upon the assumption that policy decisions have to be made in respect of set situations: that a situation has developed and remains essentially unchanged while policy-makers deliberate upon their eventual decisions. Such a view of the international environment within which policy-makers have to operate is profoundly misleading, however.

Two features of international relations render the policy context confronting policy-makers inherently dynamic. First, it is often the case that those who precipitate international development have not yet established a firm and clear view set of their aspirations and expectations. Many international situations result from actions that have an exploratory character. Second, and in a related manner, the situation that will determine whether or not any actions by a decision-maker or decision-making group will actually secure the maximum possible level of benefit for core values and objectives is not the situation that prompts the decision-making process, but the situation that will result when other states have reacted to whatever course of action is selected by the decision-maker(s) in question. The relevant situation is thus the product of a complex and dynamic process of interaction which is inherently unpredictable and cannot therefore form the basis of a value-maximising calculation of the optimal course of action. Informed guesses are often the best that are thus available to policy-makers at the time of policy choices, not the certainties required by the criteria of rational decision-making.

Problems with 'rational' decision-making

- Time is limited – a delayed decision may be a bad decision
- Effort is costly and its continued expenditure may soon bring no real improvement in decision-making
- The decision situation is fluid and dynamic, making it impossible to know what will happen before decisions are made and actions are taken

Improved group performance

If proposals for greater rationality in individual decision-making run into substantial difficulties, so too do suggestions for the improved functioning of group policy-making.

The greatest concern raised by group policy-making, particularly in the area of international relations, is the danger of group-think.[14] Simple awareness of the tendency to use social processes to generate false confidence in problematical policies is sometimes suggested as one corrective against slipping into such a potentially disastrous state of group-think. However, there are no clear criteria for differentiating the situations and policies that warrant the strong and sustained commitment of policy-makers from those that ought to be approached with greater caution and flexibility in policy-making. Indeed, group-think has all too often been used as a label with which to berate groups of policy-makers retrospectively, when their chosen policies have proven to be failures, while group-think has rarely been applied to groups of decision-makers who persevere in the face of major difficulties and ultimately secure the success of their apparently problematical policies.

More specific suggestions have also been made for the correction of tendencies towards excessive conformity within decision-making groups and over-commitment to policy options. The incorporation of a *devil's advocate* within any policy-making group has been the most popular of such suggestions. This proposal envisages the intentional involvement of individuals who are known to hold views that contrast with prevailing thinking within any decision-making group or to assign one of the existing members of the group with the role of advancing arguments that are critical of the consensus and that favour alternative lines of policy.

The problems with the devil's advocate proposal, however, derive from the very nature of decision-making groups. The social-psychological processes that often generate undue levels of consensus and conformity may also bear upon the selected devil's advocate and, if unsuccessful in bringing him, or her, to heel, lead to the effective exclusion of that individual from the effective decision-making work of the group. Moreover, once an individual is identified as the established devil's advocate, it is all to easy to dismiss his or her arguments and advice as merely a formality of no real substance: views that have to be aired for the sake of appearances but that do not require to be taken seriously.

Such qualifications notwithstanding, it clearly remains desirable to ensure that critical decision-making groups are staffed by individuals who are equipped with the widest range of pertinent knowledge, sufficiently flexible in their thinking to be able to entertain alternatives to established policies, and have strong enough personalities to resist undue pressures to conform to majority views merely because they are majority views. Much of the success of President Kennedy's *excom* group in managing the Cuban Missile Crisis[15] resulted from a membership that met these criteria. However, even in this case, it is far from clear whether the membership and 'success' of the group reflected the clear imperatives of such a potential nuclear war, rather than the wisdom or luck of President Kennedy in assembling a group of suitable quality.

Improved governmental and organisational policy-making

Improvements in the way in which wider governmental systems undertake policy-making have also attracted the attention of concerned analysts. The main focus here has been concern to avoid fragmentation within the governmental system as a whole and to overcome departmental and sectional parochiality in approach and procedure.

The establishment of link-people within each department or section of the governmental system has often been proposed as a promising path towards the reduction of fragmentation. Such people are commissioned to undertake liaison with either a single specified department or to undertake the department's liaison work in general. Such an 'open link' should ensure that the views of the department become clearly known to, and understood by, other departments and that, in turn, the positions of other departments are fully understood within the home department.

Liaison officers are, in fact, widely employed within complex governmental organisations. Their success in combating fragmentation and general incoherence may, however, be limited by a number of possibilities: that of the liaison officer 'going native' and merely absorbing the views of the department with, or in, which it has been assigned to work; that of the report of liaison officers to their home departments merely confirming the prejudices of that department; and that of the liaison officer being tolerated, but largely ignored, by departments with, or in, which he or she has to work.

The most popular proposal for combating the parochialities of departments and other sub-organisation of the wider governmental system is that of the circulation of personnel. This practice is common within Britain's Civil Service and Foreign and Commonwealth Office, particularly among its 'administrative grade' personnel. Parochiality can clearly be reduced through such circulation. Its ultimate success, however, may be reduced by the speed and effectiveness with which departments socialise incoming personnel with their views and preferences. A different difficulty is that the value of departmental expertise can be undermined by senior personnel who operate with a 'Civil Service view' or a 'Foreign Office view' which may override a specialised understanding of a particular policy problem or area of the international environment.

Common briefings and other forms of professional interaction can also be organised for the personnel of the governmental policy-making system. In large, complex and geographically dispersed governmental systems this may, however, be difficult, if not impossible, to organise for all but the most senior or most promising staff.

The general injunction to acquire greater information and implement improved information-processing systems is widely obeyed by governments and by the governments of advanced industrial states in particular. The proliferation of diplomatic representation, intelligence-gathering systems and of electronic surveillance exemplify this concern with enhanced information gathering and processing capability. Converting such an abundance of information into improved policy-making remains, however, a problematical matter, when individuals and groups, with all their intellectual and personal shortcomings, continue to have to play the critical role in converting information into policy decisions.

Improved international and inter-societal communication

Many of the problems of policy-making, that have been identified in this chapter, are ultimately a product of the ideas and perceptions entertained by central members of the decision-making system. Prejudices and misperceptions that are complicit in poor policy-making may, moreover, be shared by the wider community that the policy-makers serve. Many proposals for better international relations and, where necessary, conflict resolution thus emphasise improved communications between societies and individuals.

Proposals for improved international and inter-societal communications have been pitched at two levels. The most obvious level has been that of trying to correct the misperceptions of decision-makers and/or populations about the character, capabilities or intentions of other societies that they may fear. A wide range of private associations have been devoted to enhanced inter-societies contacts. Many efforts have also been directed, at both official and private levels, towards improved general flows of information about 'other' societies.[16] A variant of such endeavours have been attempts to clarify and redefine in a more positive light the issues that appear to be at stake between societies that are currently in conflict with one another: efforts to identify the 'win–win' features of situations that appear to be 'win-or-lose' to their participants.

The problems with such attempts to promote improved communications and perceptions is that they have to face the deeply entrenched views and prejudices of populations, if not of their decision-makers. It is difficult, if not impossible, to ensure effective communication with the entire membership of a society. Thus, while decision-makers and some of the better-informed members of a society may be convinced of the need for new perceptions of other societies, the general population may remain unconvinced. Such 'popular' resistance to change of ideas may, in turn, exert a profound constraint upon the ability of decision-makers to translate changed perceptions into appropriate changes in policy. The resistance of substantial sections of the Catholic and Protestant populations of Northern Ireland to the cooperative principles and arrangements envisaged in the 'Good Friday Agreement' for partnership in government exemplifies such a continuing constraint. Moreover, the problem is that if much of the population of the two sides of such a dispute do continue to fear and even hate one another, this is a reality that no amount of judicious communication may be able to dislodge or correct. Such difficulties demonstrate many of the problems concerning states and societies, that have been considered earlier in this book, and encounter some of the real difficulties created by the current presumption in favour of democratic principles and processes.

Proposals for changed ideas and perceptions can also be pitched at a different level, however. Many conflicts amongst human beings do reflect differences of interest or condition that appear to be very real and pressing: the dispute between Indonesians and the indigenous population of East Timor, for example. Radical theorists like John

Burton have, however, sought to evade this difficulty by moving their discussion of misperception to a different plane.

For advocates like John Burton, the structure of any immediate situation might be such as to appear to constitute an 'objective' conflict of interests but, when such a situation threatens basic human needs and objectives – physical security and survival, a general advance in prosperity, or the preservation of the world's fragile natural environment – then the perceptions of interest upon which such fundamentally damaging conflicts are based are, by definition, misperceptions of what is 'really in the interests' of the participants. In other words, if any apparent perception of interest leads people into conflicts that threatens most basic purposes of human beings, then those initial perceptions of interest must actually be misperceptions.[17]

In industrial relations, an example of Burton's view would be a situation in which workers and employers so perceive their interests that they precipitate, through their joint actions, a costly and damaging strike. Burton would argue, in such a situation, that the perceptions of conflicting interests that generated the mutually damaging strike was thus a misperception of the real interests of both sides. Many conflicts in international and inter-societal relations would be attributed to comparable misperceptions of interests by analysts who follow John Burton's approach.

The major difficulty with the Burton approach to misperception and conflict is that it ultimately requires the replacement (or supersession) of the values and perceived interests of participants in a conflict by those of the conflict-resolving analyst. There are both empirical and ethical grounds to argue that the members of some societies may prefer death to an accommodation (however peaceful ultimately) with a society and a system of values that they find fundamentally abhorrent. Similar arguments can apply to any value (and associated perception) that conflict-resolution analysts wish to propose as fundamental (and hence more real) for humanity and to supersede those actually entertained by the populations of conflicting societies.

Normative problems with the Burton approach to inter-societal communications and perceptions and, hence, to conflict resolution, complement the clear practical difficulties of advancing such alternative views in a way that is persuasive to those populations, embedded, as they are, within societies that operate to sustain and reinforce 'traditional' views and values.

Conclusions

Individuals, groups and organisations have a clear and critical role in the shaping of international relations. Individuals may aspire to rational decision-making, but are seriously constrained in this objective by intellectual limitations and contextual constraints. Policy-making in groups can provide compensation for some of the intellectual shortcomings of individual decision-makers, but add their own difficulties and dangers, particularly those associated with group-think. The wider governmental system of most modern states also plays a crucial role in the formation and implementation of international activity. Extensive knowledge and experience can be mobilised by, and within, such organisations, but their contribution may be compromised by the fragmentary consequences of departmental organisation and the parochiality of perspective and procedure that may flourish within departmentally differentiated systems.

Considerable intellectual effort has been devoted to the correction of the shortcomings of individual, group and organisational decision-making, particularly in the demanding arena of international relations. The selection of more suitable individual decision-makers has often been advocated, but this has proved easier in theory than in practice and also raises serious problems for established notions of democracy. Groups that include and sustain diversity of views have been proposed as the solution to the danger of group-think. The preservation of diversity, and the successful functioning of a devil's advocate, are, however, again easier in theory than in practice. Greater organisational cohesiveness through the extensive use of liaison officers, and in cross-departmental meetings, is, again, attractive but of variable practical effectiveness.

The promotion of improved international and inter-societal communication has, finally, found frequent advocacy as a means of correcting dangerous and/or inappropriate perceptions amongst societies and their decision-makers. Practical proposals for improving inter-societal communications, however, run into the substantial resilience of popular views and perceptions, and the associated dilemmas posed by democratic support for antagonistic attitudes. Proposals based upon presumptions of the analyst's superior conception of what is really in the interests of people, run into problems of principle and practical persuasiveness.

Popular proposals for improving decision-making in international affairs and for enhancing the quality of international and inter-society communication all deserve serious consideration. None, however, are without their difficulties: difficulties that underlie many of the persisting problems of securing a peaceful and harmonious world.

Notes

1 For a classic review of Max Weber's ideas see: R. Bendix, *Max Weber: An Intellectual Portrait* (London: Methuen, 1959).
2 For a discussion of such interest group influence see: Frohlich and Oppenheimer, *Modern Political Economy* (Englewood Cliffs, NJ: Prentice-Hall, 19878); and D. Mueller, *Public Choice* (Cambridge: Cambridge University Press, 1979).
3 See: Ole R. Holsti, Robert C. North and Richard A. Brody, 'Perception and action in the 1914 crisis', in J. David Singer (ed.), *Quantitative International Politics* (New York: Free Press, 1968), pp. 123–58.
4 For the classic descriptive account see: Elie Abel, *The Missiles of October: The Story of the Cuban Missile Crisis 1962* (London: Mayflower-Dell, 1966); and for the classic analytical stydy see: Graham T. Allison, *Essence of Decision: Explaining the Cuban Missile Crisis* (Boston, MA: Little, Brown, 1971).
5 For a classic account of which see: David Halberstam, *The Best and the Brightest* (London: Barrie & Jackson, 1973).
6 On which, see Allison, *Essence of Decision*, chapter 1.
7 Herbert Simon, *Administrative Behavior: A Study of Decision-Making Processes in Administrative Organization* (New York: Free Press, 1945).
8 C.E. Lindblom, 'The science of muddling through', *Public Administration Review*, 19, 2 (1959): 78–88; and also: D. Braybrooke and C.E. Lindblom, *A Strategy of Decision: Policy Evaluation as a Social Process* (New York: Free Press, 1963).
9 Leon Festinger, *A Theory of Cognitive Dissonance* (Evanston, IL: Row, Peterson, 1957), and *Conflict, Decision and Dissonance* (Stanford, CA: Stanford University Press, 1964)
10 Irving L. Janis, *Victims of Groupthink* (Boston, MA: Houghton Mifflin, 1982).
11 For an effective summary of these findings see: Allison, *Essence of Decison*, chapter 3.
12 Ole R. Holsti, and A.L. George, 'The effects of stress on the performance of foreign policy-makers', *Political Science Annual*, 6 (1975): 255–319.
13 E.H. Carr, *The Twenty Years' Crisis: 1919–1939: An Introduction to the Study of International Relations* (London: Macmillan, 1939).
14 Janis, *Victims of Groupthink*.
15 On which see: Robert F. Kennedy, *Thirteen Days: A Memoir of the Cuban Missile Crisis* (New York and London: Macmillan, 1969).
16 For classical advocacy of such an approach see: John Burton, *Conflict and Communication: The Use of Controlled Communication in International Relations* (London: Macmillan; New York: Free Press, 1969).

17 See, in particular: John Burton, *Systems, States, Diplomacy and Rules* (London: Cambridge University Press, 1968); and John Burton, *World Society* (London: Cambridge University Press, 1972).

Further reading

Allison, Graham, T. *Essence of Decision Explaining the Cuban Missile Crisis* (Boston, MA: Little, Brown , 1971). The path breaking discussion of alternative modes of analysing the handling of an international crisis, like that of the Cuban Missile Crisis.

Banks, Michael (ed.), *Conflict in World Society* (Brighton: Harvester/Wheatsheaf, 1984). An interesting set of discussions within the 'world society' and conflict as misperception schools of thought.

Burton, John W., *Conflict and Communication* (London: Macmillan, 1969). A clear statement of the view that international misunderstanding and conflict are the product of human misperceptions.

Festinger, Leon, *A Theory of Cognitive Dissonance* (Evanston, IL: Row, Peterson, 1957). A seminal statement of the psychological foundations human intellectual and perceptual rigidity.

Kelman, H.C. (ed.), *International Behavior: A Social-Psychological Analysis* (New York: Holt, Rinehart & Winston, 1965). A classic collection of articles on the psychological and social psychological foundations of international conflict.

3 States, societies and international relations

Radical analysts throughout history have refused to accept that the roots of conflict amongst peoples lie within human nature itself. Critical observers, from nineteenth-century anarchists[1] through to contemporary critical theorists,[2] have argued that it is the state, as an institution, that is the real source of the apparent shortcomings of the international system. To Marxists, moreover, it was not so much the state *per se* that was the problem but the socio-economic systems within which the state had been located at different historical phases, most particularly the capitalist system within which the world's leading states were now located.[3] In essence, classical Marxists argued that capitalism was inherently exploitative and unstable and could survive only through a remorseless process of expansion that would ultimately and inevitably generate international conflict.[4] The terms of the debate here are thus clear – between those who identify the international system as the source of conflict and instability in human affairs and those who see the state, whether as an institution or as a function of flawed socio-economic systems, as the source of many of the persistent problems of world affairs.

Patterns

In terms of the international relations theory, the modern state and the system to which it gave rise, began in 1648, following the Treaty of Westphalia. This treaty had brought to an end the Thirty Years War, the great war of religion in Europe. The conflict over religion that had led to such wholesale slaughter on both sides was resolved at Westphalia by the establishment of the principle that each state would follow the religion of its ruler. Thus, from that time onwards states tended to concern themselves with relations between each other that were based on political rather than religious factors.[5]

States had existed before the Thirty Years War. Most centuries had seen the progressive centralisation of power in the hands of a single ruler or a ruling oligarchy and the steady spread of the jurisdiction of a central government. Thus, states and a centralised authority with internal and external sovereignty were in existence before the Thirty Years War began. However, the process advanced substantially after 1648. Post Westphalia the role of the state underwent a distinct change. Increasingly, states would now be expected to meet the needs of the citizens in a number of ways. They would have a primary duty to defend the area of land that they occupied and to protect the citizens from invasion and other external disruption. In addition, the state's government would provide the means of enforcing law and order at home in such a way that the prosperity and economic well-being of the citizens could be maintained and improved. Finally, the state gradually acquired an obligation to provide for the welfare and living standards of all its citizens. In return for providing security for its population in these areas, the state required the loyalty of the citizens living within its boundaries. Over time, the citizens of these states began to identify themselves more closely with the state in which they lived and to develop concepts of common purpose and a common history that would identify them as a nation.

The concept of the state, however, often has a somewhat indiscriminate implication. In practice, it has always been clear that not all states are equal in power and influence. Great powers have generally had global interests and global capabilities and their actions could have far-reaching and important consequences for almost every member of the global system. Examples of great powers in the seventeenth, eighteenth and nineteenth centuries would be Britain, France, Austria-Hungary. By contrast, small powers had very limited capabilities and were often chiefly concerned with survival and with their relationship to immediate neighbours. An example of a small power in the seventeenth, eighteenth and nineteenth centuries would be Poland.

Since the Second World War, three other types of state have also been identified: regional powers, superpowers and micro-states. First there are regional powers; states whose interests have been primarily within their own geographical regions and whose capabilities have generally limited them to such an arena. Britain and France would be good examples of regional powers in the context of the late twentieth early twenty-first century. Second, there are superpowers which became a phenomenon of the post-1945 Cold War period which was dominated by the Soviet Union and the United States. These states not only had global interests and capabilities but also had the added capacity of a huge arsenal of nuclear weapons, capable of destroying all other states on earth, including other superpowers. Finally, and very much at the other extreme, come a large grouping of micro-states. States in this category are often regarded as being small or relatively insignificant but capable of sustaining some form of separate existence. States that have emerged following the end of the Cold War and the break up of the former Soviet Union, Micronesia in the Pacific and island communities such as the Picturing Islands or St Helena, although these last two remain British colonies.

The chapter on the international system considers the view that the structure of the international system – the number and distributional patterns of powers of different types – might have a significant bearing upon the frequency and intensity of international conflict. A focus on the level of the state and/or society, however, delves beneath general structural features to ask whether states are always inherently aggressive, whether different kinds of states (dictatorships or democracies, for instance) are more or less likely to be aggressive internationally, and whether different kinds of socio-economic systems, or even cultures, have different implications for international peace and stability. Critical to such a discussion is the recognition that not all states have participated in armed international conflict at all times and that individual states have varying records of involvement in different forms and levels of aggressive international behaviour.

Sources

It should be clear that over the past centuries since the Treaty of Westphalia the nature of states in the context of international politics has changed considerably. As has already been noted, citizens increasingly identified themselves with their own state, and a feeling of nationalism and nationhood developed.[6] As technology increased the likelihood that more citizens would be affected by war, identification with the state and its interests grew stronger. Individuals took on a societal attitude and often placed their own interests below those of the state, which often expressed its foreign policy in terms of the national interest. It is worth noting at this point that the efforts of organisations like the Socialist International to reject loyalty to the nation in favour of class loyalty fell on deaf ears as massive numbers of working-class people flocked to join up to fight against their country's enemies at the outbreak of the First World War. This suggests that by 1914 there was a high degree of identity between all citizens within the state and that state's interests. Furthermore it marked an apparent rejection of three other interpretations. The first was that the state is an artificial and repressive construction, which is devised by and for a self-interested minority and which is imposed upon a malleable populace through a wide range of institutionalised agencies, including the church, the educational system and cultural creations. The second was the view that divisions within societies, and divisions along class lines, are far more important than any divisions amongst states and societies. The third interpretation that seemed to be rejected by the development of the nation state was the idea of a world, or global, society in which people with similar interests would be united across the artificial boundaries of the state. State boundaries, however artificial they might appear to be, proved to be effective in identifying groups with shared ideals and interests, and, for good or ill, differentiated one group from another.[7]

As a consequence of the war experiences of the early part of the twentieth century, however, the role of the state has been subject to increasing challenge. The development of devastating weapons and equally devastating means of delivering such weapons has meant that the state can rarely fulfil its obligations to protect its citizens in times of total war. The invention of the bomber, the strategy of aerial bombardment and the deployment of atomic and nuclear weapons have all been examples of changes that have led to threats to the 'territoriality of the state'. States have also come under threat from the economic activities of multi-national enterprises which have been able to exploit resources at will and undermine the ability of states to manage their own economies. The development of larger economic markets, such as the Single European Market, have further undermined the ability of individual states to look after the economic or welfare interests of their citizens and have posed a further threat to their very existence.

Finally, with the expansion of the number of states within the international system a small group of states have collapsed into domestic anarchy and civil war, and are failing in their general obligations to their citizens. States such as Somalia and Ethiopia are examples of this phenomenon. What remains surprising, however, is that so many people have expended so much energy and effort, and sometimes violence, to gain statehood and independence for themselves and their fellow countrymen. Whether an anarchical system imposes an imperative for self-help upon societies, or whether the self-regarding state creates an anarchical condition within the 'international' system, the clear importance of sovereignty and control over one's own destiny retains a fundamental hold over a large number of peoples.

In addition to the description of states in terms of their size and influence in respect of international relations, some analysts have also considered the role of domestic structures in the making of a state's foreign policy. In this context states have been classified as much by their governmental structure and their level of social cohesion as by their size and influence. States can thus be differentiated in terms of a number of central variables. The first variable would be that ranging from democracy to despotism. The implications of democratic government will be discussed further later in this chapter. In despotic states, however, it is generally assumed that decisions are made by a single individual or a very small oligarchy, often without regard to the views or interests of the population as a whole. A second key variable is that of the level of cohesion of the state. This has often reflected the historical experience of the state and the degree of national loyalty to the state's institutions. States in which there is a high degree of national unity have generally been regarded as more effective than those that lack this ingredient. Cohesive states might also be regarded as likely to be more peace loving. In contrast, states may exhibit a high degree of tension and disorder, which may be caused either by ethnic tensions, by general dissatisfaction with the system of government or by longer-term institutional weaknesses in the system of government and the supporting political culture. While some states may, as a consequence of internal divisions, become entirely dysfunctional and effectively cease to play the role of a state, other states' leaders have attempted to adopt a more aggressive foreign policy in an effort to create, however temporarily, a feeling of national well-being and unity. These efforts sometimes involved the creation of real or imagined enemies in an effort to force people to unite to rebuff the threat of external invasion. State leaders that pursued this approach have sometimes found that, when a real attack does take place, their appeals for unity or external assistance fall on deaf ears.

The persisting characteristic of modern international relations is that all states exhibit a concern with the interests of their citizens and subjects, and that these interests are often expressed in terms of

States and external behaviour: possible key domestic variables

Democracy ——	Despotism
Cohesion ——	Division

exercising power and influence over other states within the international system. On the other hand, there may often be interests and objects in common amongst states and cooperation to achieve these common goals. Whatever the reason for the adoption of a particular approach, in many states there is a tendency for citizens or subjects to allow the government to define foreign policy objectives as part of its executive function. The effect of this is that, more often than not, the leaders of states believe that as sovereign entities they are free to act as they think fit in their relations with other states, irrespective of the views of the citizens.

The criticism of an emphasis upon the domestic sources of international conduct, made primarily by system-level theorists, is that domestic politics are or at least should be a veneer. Realists, in particular, tend to argue that the sound and fury that often accompanies foreign policy-making actually rarely amounts to much because states do end up making decisions that lead them to pursue their national interests. And, on those rare occasions when they do not, the results are typically disastrous. Scholars who focus on the state as their level of analysis obviously, however, argue that the determination of a state's external activity is so complex as to make such an interpretation of international conduct highly simplistic.

Although neither systems-level theorists nor state-level analysts have ever tried to assess the relative impact of the systemic and state factors definitively, empirical evidence suggests that the Realist's view, when expressed in its simplest terms, is at best overstated. Studies of everything from critical events such as the Cuban Missile Crisis[8] to less earth-shattering decisions such as the Blair Labour government's adoption of a more ethical dimension in foreign policy[9] show that, at least as far as individual decisions are concerned, domestic politics often make a tremendous difference in determining what happens. It may be that those forces balance each other when long-term and world-wide trends are considered, but the real world of politics is based on decisions made on individual issues.

The central and continuing issue for students of international relations is that the end of the wars of religion in the seventeenth century did not see the end of war. Although military actions after 1648 were fought for rather different reasons, wars continued to dominate international relations. The main purpose of these conflicts was either to retain or overthrow the existing balance of power or to prevent any single state from gaining total dominance. Wars thus became an instrument of political policy rather than conflicts of ideology; less intense but still comparatively frequent. As will be seen in the next chapter, it was only when wars became more ideological and intense, and the dividing lines between states became clearer, that semi-permanent alliances between states were established. When this occurred there was a return to more bloody and ideological warfare.

The role of nationalism

After the ideological upheavals of the Napoleonic wars there was an attempt to return to the *ancien regime*: the previous patterns of political conduct and the values and beliefs by which they were underpinned. However, the nineteenth century saw the rise of a new threat to the stability of the international system. This time the threat came from within the states themselves. The emergence of nationalism as a potential force posed a significant threat to the stability of the system and the nature of states.[10] Many national communities that felt themselves to be discriminated against, or ruled over, by an alien culture sought independence from imperial regimes or dominating governments.

In the early years of the eighteenth century in South America, for example, the exploits of leaders such as Simon Bolivar were instrumental in the liberation of the states of that region from Spanish or Portuguese rule. The same period in Europe also saw democratic and/or nationalist revolutionaries acting against autocratic regimes and the multi-national empires of Austria-Hungary and Turkey with mixed success. The ultimate collapse of the old system came in 1919 with the end of the First World War, which was accompanied by the triumph of nationalism and the adoption of the principle of national self-determination at the Treaty of Versailles. States were now viewed as the product of democratic and liberal principles, with the principle of self-determination underpinning the dawn of the true nation state. Henceforth, nation states would now reflect the concerns of groups who would feel themselves to be united by common interests and concerns, which would make it easier for them to work together.[11] The causes of conflict would therefore be reduced as the principles of democracy were enhanced. Few of those who endorsed the liberal nationalism of the inter-war era could have anticipated, at the time, that the ultimate effect of their actions would be to create a system that would last for less than twenty years, experience almost permanent crisis and end in a second, even more devastating world war.

Revolutionary statism

It is somewhat ironic that, against the background of liberal nationalism at the end of the First World War, there was a second revolutionary change, but this time one that was committed to a rather different set of principles. In 1917 the Bolshevik revolution against the then Provisional Government of Russia (the short-lived successor to the Imperial, Tsarist government) brought Lenin and the Communist party to power. This change of governmental system brought with it an entirely different view of the role of the state. There was a belief that the revolution in Russia would spark a series of further revolutions that would lead to the triumph of the proletariat. Once this was achieved all existing states would 'wither away' and be replaced by a kind of Communist Commonwealth. In the meantime, however, the Dictatorship of the Proletariat required that the state should be revivified and that the individual interest of citizens should be subordinated to those of the state. This concept reversed the traditional liberal view that the state should be the servant of the citizen.

However the idea that the purposes and power of the state were of greater importance than those of the citizens, in whose interests it supposedly governed, was not just a left-wing phenomenon. This view was, to a large extent, shared by those on the extreme right of politics, who espoused the cause of fascism and Nazism. The elevation and development of the nation-state enabled leaders, such as Adolf Hitler in the 1930s, not just to impose dictatorial rule but also, by means of 'perverted science', to attempt to elevate some nationalities over others. In justifying their efforts to achieve racial purity, fascist leaders placed an exaggerated emphasis on the differences rather than the similarities between, and even sometimes within, the populations of states. This led to intense conflict and ultimately war.

The disorder that surrounded the period between the two world wars was thus attributed by many liberal theorists to the fact that there were too many undemocratic states and that these were the kind of 'bad' states which would cause wars.

Socio-economic pathologies

In contrast to an emphasis upon the causal role of the overblown state, the Marxist analysis, which was adopted by the Soviet Union and by states sympathetic to it, argued that the causes of war arose from an entirely different origin. Marxists argued that war was indeed the consequence of some states being 'bad'. However, to them a 'bad' state was a capitalist state and it was these states that were the primary cause of conflict and war. This was because of the inherent nature of capitalism with its constant need to expand into newer and ever-larger markets as a means of maintaining and increasing profits. Capitalists were also involved in a constant search for scarce raw materials to feed the ever-expanding industrial system over which they presided. The struggle to acquire secure markets and new sources of raw materials led to the development of empires which led, in turn, to conflict amongst capitalist nations. Imperialism was, to the Marxist, the final stage of capitalism. This approach was based on an earlier liberal analysis by J.A. Hobson whose book, *Imperialism,*[12] had argued much the same point. The dialectical process of thesis, antithesis and synthesis, together with the inevitability of history, were thus bound up in the process that would lead to major conflicts amongst competing capitalist countries and, indeed, to a final conflict between capitalism and communism, from which the latter would emerge triumphant.

Marxists, therefore, argued that the answer to the problem of war was the abolition of capitalism and that once this was achieved world peace would, in all likelihood, be established. A world proletariat society would be established that would harmonise the interests of all within a Communist Commonwealth. It was generally accepted that, even after the establishment of a Communist Commonwealth, conflicts and disagreements would still arise but that these, unlike those of previous systems, would be non-antagonistic and would be resolved through the dialectic process.

Pathologies of society and political system

The Marxist focus upon the socio-economic causes of international conflict is, however, merely one, basically mono-causal, interpretation of the sources of external aggressiveness that might lie within individual states. A wider political/cultural interpretation has also been developed which attributes international aggressiveness to shortcomings in the general culture prevailing within a society (an enculturalised emphasis upon personal aggressiveness and/or a militaristic philosophy for example)[13] or, as will be seen subsequently, the failure to develop mature and durable forms of democratic governance. Even more specific explanations of the outbreak of international aggressiveness have, however, been sought in a general tendency for human beings (along with most advanced animals) to act aggressively when faced with actual, or perceived, threats to basic values – the Dollard–Doob frustration–aggression hypothesis.[14]

In conclusion it is clear that a considerable number of analysts of the causes of war have placed great emphasis on the internal structures of states as primary causes of war. They have used their analyses to attempt to prove that certain kinds of states are 'bad' and that, if the changes they advocated were to be adopted, most problems between states, if such continued to exist, would disappear. However, any mono-causal analysis of such a complex subject as war is bound to be oversimplified and leave out many other factors that may contribute to incidents of violent conflict. Therefore, a wider analysis of the causes of conflict needs to be developed. Such an analysis would have to include some assessment of factors such as human nature, the capacity of individual humans under pressure to make mistakes, the possibility of success if military force is used, the irrationality of some individuals in positions of power, non-conformity of individuals to the 'rules of the game', as well as the lack of restraint emanating from the international system taken as a whole.

The geo-political conditions of states

The existence of states and the definition of their territory, along with the growing feeling amongst their citizens and subjects of belonging to a territorially defined social and political entity, all contribute to a view of the world that has been increasingly ethno-centric and to wider interpretations that emphasise geographical influences upon international politics.[15] The leaders and populations of states tend to see the world through the perspective of a particular view of their position within it and as a result of their historical experience. However, this perception of themselves and their place is not always shared by others.

The former Soviet Union was, for example, a large state stretching over many thousands of miles and seemingly impregnable. The government of that country was, nevertheless, constantly concerned with the need to ensure that secure frontiers were in existence. To the Soviet leadership the experiences dating back to Tsarist times and the Napoleonic wars if not before, along with the experiences of the First World War, the anti-Communist Intervention and Hitler's invasion, all pointed to the need for a defensible and secure frontier. To the external observer, however, every attempt to invade the territory occupied by the Soviet state over many hundreds of years had foundered, often as a result of the harsh climate or the logistics involved in sustaining such an invasion. There were thus differing views about whether the defence of Russia against its enemies really had to be the priority for Soviet leaders. On its side, however, the Soviet leadership could point to a succession of threats, from interventions to try to reverse the Bolshevik revolution after 1917; invasion by Nazi Germany in 1941; and the post-war emergence of confrontations with NATO, Communist China and Islamic Fundamentalism.

A parallel concern of Russian and Soviet leaders has also been the lack of warm water ports along its coastline. Thus the world view from Moscow was of a country surrounded by enemies and in desperate need of an aggressive defence capability in order to ensure the continued existence of the Soviet governmental system. This approach was interpreted by other states as an example of a state hell-bent on expansionism and world aggression. The fact that states fail to fully appreciate each other's point of view may thus also be seen as a primary cause of conflict and war.[16]

The possibility that the leaders and populations of one state may not see the world in the same way as the leaders and peoples of other states also illustrates the problem with geo-political influences. Geography clearly exists, but its significance will be altered by changing circumstances (the advent of military aircraft reducing the significance of such traditional barriers as rivers) and by altered perceptions (an exposed border with a perceived friend being far less worrying than such a frontier with a long-term adversary).

Complexity and the state and/or society as causes of international conflict

THE PROBLEM

The end of the Cold War did not bring about the triumph of democracy or the period of sustained peace that might have been anticipated. This again suggests that the causes of war are more deep-seated than those offered by simplistic, mono-causal analyses of the problem. Indeed, the end of the Cold War stimulated, rather than reduced, the incidence of conflict and war, as civil wars, wars of separation and simple nationalistic wars all erupted shortly after 1990. Never have either the UN or other military and political institutions been so busy as they were in the immediate post-Cold War period. International opinion has been angered by the return of 'ethnic cleansing' and of extremists apparently determined to make their state 'pure' and to eliminate from their societies any who do not meet the necessary criteria for membership. Despite this, and in a more hopeful vein, it might be possible to conclude that war is something that *may* occur rather than something that always *will* occur. The problem is we have not yet found the right formula for resolving international conflicts peacefully, despite the time and efforts that theorists of international politics have devoted to establishing what it is about the state that could possibly lead it to fight wars and involve itself in conflict.

Democratic peace theory

A key proposition that arose from many of the past attempts to analyse the causes of war was that wars are caused by 'bad' states. Simple though this proposition might appear, it is obvious that the definition of precisely what constitutes a 'bad' state is the subject of considerable controversy. If it could be shown that states that are democratic are inherently more peaceful than states that are not and that states with greater social cohesion are similarly more likely to adopt a peaceful approach to international relations, then the definition of a 'bad' state would be clear and obvious. In the view of 'liberal' thinkers on international politics war is an irrational act and democracy by its very nature is rational. The global adoption of democracy as a form of government should ensure that peaceful relations are maintained in the international system. Wars could only be caused in this analysis by the few remaining undemocratic states or states whose governments did not reflect or acknowledge public opinion. The problem of war could thus most easily be solved by making the world 'safe for democracy' and encouraging the establishment of a global system of democratic states. This raises a key question that is today one of the hottest and most controversial issues in academic circles today – democratic peace theory.[17]

Democratic peace theory: variants

- Democracies do not go to war
- Democracies do not start wars
- Democracies do not go to war with one another

The simplest version of democratic peace theory states that democracies are inherently pacific and do not, in particular, initiate violence against other societies. The truth of this proposition depends, however, upon the way in which democracies are defined (what are the critical criteria and how long are such democracies supposed to have been in existence?) and the definition of inter-societal violence (should it include armed subversion, the support for local rebels within another country?).[18]

In the second variant of democratic peace theory it is argued that, even if the problems of defining democracies and inter-state violence do raise considerable problems, democracies, nevertheless, never enter into armed conflict with one another. This second variant of the theory, however, encounters exactly the same problems of definition and identification of both the true nature of democracy and the specification of armed conflict as those encountered by the simplest version.

The third, and most refined version of democratic peace theory asserts that it is only 'liberal democracies' that never go to war with one another. This proposition is a little more manageable definitionally (liberal democracies having such characteristics as adult suffrage, regular elections, regular changes of government by peaceful means, parliamentary control of the executive and the general rule of law) and stands up fairly well against the historical record. It is also important to be clear that liberal democracies do fight wars. Indeed, the United States fought more wars than any other country during the twentieth century. As recently as the 1980s, Great Britain went to war with Argentina over the Falkland/Malvinas Islands. And, most recently, most of the world's democracies banded together to take on Iraq following its invasion of Kuwait in August 1990. In even more recent times, action has also been taken in Bosnia over Kosovo and in Indonesia following the East Timor referendum on independence.

Democratic peace: possible explanations

- Democratic governments are restrained by their citizens/voters
- Democratic governments favour discussion and negotiated agreements of disputes
- Democratic governments are concerned with the preservation of economic well-being

However, the point being stressed here is that liberal democracies have not fought each other in recent years no matter how tense their relations. There are instances in which pre-modern democracies (e.g., Greek city states 2,500 years ago) went to war. There are also some ambiguous cases (was the Confederacy democratic, and, if so, does that make the US Civil War of 1861–5 a war between democracies; and was the war between Britain and the Boer republic at the turn of the nineteenth and twentieth centuries a war between democracies of a sort?). On balance, however, the evidence during the last decades of the twentieth century, that liberal democracies do not fight each other, has been firmer than many other trends in the social sciences.[19]

By contrast, non-democratic regimes tend to be both more war-prone and more ruthless once they start fighting. Thus, the most conventionally aggressive countries in the twentieth century were also the least democratic, although it is important to recall that Adolf Hitler's Nazi party was elected democratically within Germany's inter-war Weimar Republic. Perhaps more importantly, there is some, albeit less overwhelming, evidence that when democracies do go to war they inflict fewer casualties on civilians and troops than non-democratic governments.

Critics of the democratic peace think it is a classic example of a spurious correlation. Democracies may not fight each other, but the reasons for this are altogether different and have little or nothing to do with democracy. From their perspective, the mislabelled democratic peace could be a product of the particular circumstances of the last two hundred years, cultural similarities between the liberal democracies, a function of capitalism rather than of political systems, of general economic prosperity or, frankly, of just plain luck. The biggest (and currently unanswered) question confronting liberal democratic peace theory is thus whether the maintenance of liberal democracies and their relatively peaceful international dispositions are the result of other, underlying factors, and, hence, whether the correlation between liberal democracy and mutual non-aggression will break down if there are significant changes in any of the underlying factors.

Problems with democratic peace theory

- The precise definition of a democracy – all democracies or only liberal democracies?
- The unambiguous definition of war, aggression, etc.
- The prosperous, status quo character of the majority of contemporary democracies
- The durability of democracies and, hence, of any associated peace

Problems

States and societies have thus been seen to create many of the most serious sources of international conflict throughout modern history. The connection of both states and societies with war and conflict remains, however, a complex and controversial matter, as does the connection between states and their component societies: do delinquent and aggressive states reflect shortcomings in the society that they represent, or are flawed societies and cultures created under the influence of wayward states?

The abolition of the state is, as has been seen, a preferred option for many critical theorists, particularly from the time of the French Revolution. The problem with this prescription, however, can be identified through a further question: has the emergence of the modern state been an unfortunate accident in human development, or has it developed as the primary mechanism for ensuring social order and stability and the provision of a range of desirable services for the community that it serves? If the modern state does fulfil some essential functions, when it is operating as it should, then the weakening or abolition of the state might merely create more problems than they would solve. The improvement of the state, particularly where it is weak or malfunctioning, might then prove to be the most fruitful way forward for humanity.

Societies that display undue levels of aggressiveness also create problems for those who would reduce the incidence of international conflict and place international relations on a permanently peaceful footing. The practical difficulties of influencing the social and cultural foundations that underpin the international dispositions of other peoples are the first problems encountered by such a manipulative strategy. Ethical and inter-cultural issues are also raised by such endeavours: what right does one group of people have to criticise and to try and 'correct' the supposed social and cultural shortcomings of others, when those 'shortcomings' may actually represent long-standing, deeply embedded and highly valued principles and practices.

Identifying the sources of international conflict in the economic systems of states creates comparable problems. The practical problems of exerting a positive influence upon the economic systems of other states are considerable, particularly when they are market economies, characterised by highly dispersed decision-making and sources of power and influence. Persuading or compelling people to transform the principles upon which they base their economic lives will also encounter considerable practical problems (as the efforts of Green campaigners have experienced).

The resolution of such practical and ethical problems when seeking to modify the states, societies or economic systems of other peoples has encouraged more modest approaches to the encouragement of international peace and harmony based upon the support of suitable social movements and the promotion of greater political democratisation.

Solutions

Social movements

On balance observers are coming to the conclusion that expansion of public participation makes it harder for elites to lead their countries in rash and aggressive directions. Perhaps more importantly, social movements have been largely responsible for putting many of the issues covered in other chapters on to the world's political agenda. It is useful to recall some of them here.

The 1997 Nobel Peace Prize was awarded to the International Committee for the Abolition of Land Mines. Six months later, a UN commission was engaged in negotiations that would lead to the creation of an International Criminal Court and included rape as one of other war crimes under its jurisdiction. These issues were raised not by conventional, established experts but by grass roots activists. These are not just phenomena of the political left. Conservative organisations in Britain and the United States have effectively organised resistance that led their governments to slow down movement toward further and more rapid regional economic integration.

In short, the argument here is one found in discussions of democratic – and especially American – politics since the Federalists wrote their famous papers in defence of the constitution during the debate over its ratification in the late 1780s. They responded to the then common fear that any single group or 'faction' could amass too much power and impose its will over the rest of the society. The Federalists argued that the 'evils of faction' were most prominent in small jurisdictions like the then thirteen states. The creation of a larger and more pluralistic state, in which dozens of groups competed against each other, would, in their version, lead to policy making via compromise in which each group got a piece of the 'political pie' and could not dominate. More generally, an open and democratic system maximises the chances of groups, like the Committee to Ban Land mines, having an influence at all stages of the policy process, from first getting an issue on to the agenda to seeing treaties and other formal legal conventions implemented.

The history of the environmental movement in the United States illustrates the exercise of such influence. In the late 1960s, there were few environmental groups, and none of them were taken seriously. Organisations from the political mainstream (the World Resources Institute) and those further out of the political spectrum (Greenpeace) continued to work, however, with two consequences. First, more and more people became concerned about deteriorating environmental conditions, and, second, more and more pressure was exerted upon the US government to change its policies at home and abroad. By the time of the Rio Summit in 1992, US policy-makers had to cooperate with the unofficial delegation of NGOs which was dramatically to the Bush administration's environmental left. When President Clinton took office, he turned to the more moderate environmental organisations for experts to fill some of the hundred or so environmental positions in his administration.

Some observers also advocate the expanded use of less formal forms of diplomacy – including citizen diplomacy – which only became a significant part of international relations in the last two decades and which carry considerable promise for bringing societies as well as governments into more cooperative relationships.

Democratisation

Even more popular now are proposals to expand democracy to more of the world and to deepen it where it has established roots.[20] The advocates of democratisation accept many of the critiques of democratic peace theory and do not assume that greater political democracy is a panacea for the world's problems. However, there is enough evidence of links between democracy and the protection of human rights, support for the status of women and minorities, and environmentalism – though perhaps not equitable economic development – that a growing number of states and NGOs are stressing democratisation as an important mission for the international community.

It is also widely accepted that democratisation is a long and complicated process. In the West, it took hundreds of years and involved many setbacks and considerable violence in all the countries that seem stable and democratic today. It is hoped, however, that the process can be speeded up and smoothed out in the third world and former Soviet bloc.

Equally wide is the acknowledgement that democratisation involves more than the just the adoption of a liberal constitution that guarantees basic political freedoms and stipulates that rulers will be chosen through fair and competitive elections, it also involves more intangible developments that could well be more important than any constitutional provisions. Such measures include the development of a civil society – the groups and institutions that exist to fulfil a range of social functions beyond the direct purview of the government – toleration of opposing viewpoints, acceptance of the rule of law and, simply, a degree of experience through which a consensus about the rules of the political game can emerge.[21]

Despite the considerable difficulties of imposing democracy from abroad, many Western governments, development agencies and NGOs have put democratisation at or near the top of their list of foreign policy priorities. There is nothing new in the concern with democratisation, and a concern for democracy has featured prominently in US foreign policy for at least a century. However, many concerns in the past, including those of the Cold War, have often driven democratisation down Washington's list of priorities.

The end of the Cold War has made it easier for the international community to promote democracy for two reasons. First, the collapse of communism in Europe and Central Asia means that there has been no serious competitor to democracy (and capitalism) in world political life. Second, Western governments and aid agencies simply have had more time and resources to devote to democratisation and other goals.

The push for democratisation has thus become one of those global forces impinging on both state and society. Attempts to pressure states to adopt democratic institutions and practices are, however, more visible than those aimed at developing civil society and toleration. There is not yet any discernible pattern to those efforts at democratisation, and all we can do is point out a few illustrative examples.

Some instances of pressure have involved military force. For example, in 1994, under the formal aegis of the United Nations, the United States threatened to use force to oust military dictator Raoul Cedras from power in Haiti and return the elected Bertrand Aristide to the presidency. In fact, troops were already in the air before Cedras agreed to step down in the negotiations with an American delegation headed by Senator Sam Nunn and former President Jimmy Carter. US troops remained in the country to restore order during the transition back to civilian rule and to train Haitians in maintaining law and order within a democracy.

Other attempts to promote democracy have involved the threat of force, but not of a military nature. Increasingly the Bretton Woods institutions and governments are applying conditionality before granting further aid and loans. In the 1980s and the first half of the 1990s, they insisted that recipient governments adopt liberal economic policies known as structural adjustment – policies designed to restore balance in the public finances and to favour the free-market development of states that are recipients of financial aid. In the late 1990s, they have added political strings to the aid as well. The most important recent example came during the economic crisis that swept East Asia during 1997 and 1998 and hit Indonesia particularly hard.[22] The IMF took the lead in insisting that the Indonesian government respect basic human and political rights as part of its bail-out package, a demand that ultimately led to the downfall of President Suharto, who had been in power for thirty years.

Some attempts at influence have involved gentler forms of persuasion and probably had less of an impact as a result. In 1993, Chief Moshood Abiola apparently won a presidential election that was to mark the transition from military to civilian rule in Nigeria. The government annulled the results and imprisoned Abiola shortly thereafter. The international community imposed some sanctions, including reduction in economic aid and a ban on Nigerian athletes participating in African competitions. The United States, the Commonwealth of Nations and the Organisation of African Unity also tried to exert diplomatic pressure on the military to improve its horrendous human rights record and hasten the return to civilian government. Those efforts increased following the sudden, unexpected, and, some believe, suspicious deaths of military strong man Sani Abacha and Abiola.

Less visible, but perhaps more important for the long term have been attempts to bolster support for democracy in such societies. Almost all Western governments are increasingly giving aid to projects that will help develop civil society. The United States' Agency for International Development (USAID) is pumping tens of millions of dollars a year into such projects.

It is far too early to assess democratisation, because it is not yet possible to tell whether two important things will occur. First, it is by no means clear that the current wave of democratisation in Latin America, parts of Africa and East Asia will last. Given economic pressures, particularly within Asia and Africa, and given the impatience of many persistently poor people who are suffering more than ever, partly as a result of the structural adjustment programs imposed by the same Western countries, it is by no means certain that these new democracies will survive. Second, it is also by no means certain that democracy alone will be enough to ensure the beneficial international outcomes that have come so far as a result of the processes posited in the arguments about the democratic peace. As noted earlier, it could well be that what looks like a link between democracy and peace may be the result of some wholly different third fact (e.g., Western cultural similarities, or the fact that most of the mature democracies are also rich and economically prosperous societies) and, thus, may not operate in the rest of the world. Nonetheless, democratisation is firmly on the world's political agenda and seems likely to stay there for the foreseeable future.

Notes

1 For summaries of Anarchist theory see: George Woodcock, *Anarchism: A History of Libertarian Ideas and Movements* (Harmondsworth: Penguin Books, 1963); and April Carter, *The Political Theory of Anarchism* (London: Routledge & Kegan Paul, 1971).
2 See, for instance, Richard K. Ashley, 'Political realism and human interests', *International Studies Quarterly*, 25, 2 (June 1981): 204–36; and Richard K. Ashley, 'The poverty of neo-realism', *International Organization*, 38, 2 (Spring 1984): 225–61.
3 For a succinct statement of this conventional 'Marxist' view see: Ralph Miliband, *The State in Capitalist Society: The Analysis of the Western System of Power* (London: Weidenfeld & Nicolson, 1973).
4 See: A. Brewer, *Marxist Theories of Imperialism* (London: Routledge & Kegan Paul, 1980).
5 For an interesting recent discussion of the Westphalian order, see: David L. Blaney and Naeem Inayatullak, 'The Westphalian deferral', *International Studies Review*, 2, 2 (Summer, 2000): 29–64
6 For an interesting discussion see: James Mayall, *Nationalism and International Society* (Cambridge: Cambridge University Press, 1990).
7 For a wide ranging examination of the 'state' see: James A. Caporaso (ed.), *The Elusive State: International and Comparative Perspectives* (Newbury Park, CA: Sage, 1989).
8 On which, see: Graham T. Allison, *The Essence of Decision* (Boston, MA: Little, Brown, 1971).
9 On which see: Jim Buller, 'New Labour's foreign and defence policy: external support structures and domestic politics', in S. Ludlam and M.J. Smith (eds), *New Labour in Government* (Houndmills: Macmillan, 2001), pp. 234–55, esp. pp. 229–31.
10 For a survey of the situation during the late nineteenth century, see: Norman Stone, *European Transformed 1878–1919* (London: Fontana, revised edn, 1984), esp. pp. 107–28.
11 See: Anthony D. Smith, *National Identity* (Harmondsworth: Penguin Books, 1991).
12 J.A. Hobson, *Imperialism: A Study* (Ann Arbor, MI: University of Michigan Press, 1905).
13 See, for example, Albert Bandura, *Aggression: A Social Learning Analysis* (Englewood Cliffs, NJ: Prentice Hall, 1973). And for a general view that contrasting cultures (or civilisations) will form the major fracture line of future international conflicts see: Samuel P. Huntingdon, *The Clash of Civilizations and the Remaking of World Order* (New York: Simon & Schuster, 1996).
14 John Dollard and Leonard W. Doob, *et al., Frustration and Aggression* (New Haven, CT: Yale University Press, 1939).
15 There has been a long tradition of 'geo-politics', outstanding examples being: A.T. Mahon, *The Influence of Sea Power upon History 1660–1783* (London: Methuen, 1965, originally published in 1890); and Halford J. MacKinder, *Democratic Ideals and Reality: A Study of the Politics of Reconstruction* (New York: Henry Holt, 1919).

16 For a classic statement of which see: Uri Bronfenbrenner, 'The mirror image in Soviet–American relations: a social psychologist's report', *Journal of Social Issues*, 17, 3 (1961): 45–56.

17 On democratic peace theory see: Michael Doyle, 'Kant, liberal legacies and foreign policy, Parts I and II', *Philosophy and Public Affairs*, 12 (1983): 205–35 and 323–53; Bruce Russett, *Grasping the Democratic Peace: Principles for a Post-Cold War World* (Princeton, NJ: Princeton University Press, 1993); for a critical view see: Raymond Cohen, 'Pacific unions: a reappraisal of the theory that "democracies do not go to war with each other"', *Review of International Studies*, 20 (1994): 207–23; and for a recent overview see: Thomas Risse-Kappen (ed.), 'Special issue: democracy and peace', *European Journal of International Relations* (1995).

18 See, in particular, Cohen, 'Pacific Unions'.

19 Thomas Risse-Kappen (ed.), 'Special issue: democracy and peace'.

20 For a seminal review of the conditions for developing democracy see: Adam Przeworski *et al.*, *Sustainable Democracy* (Cambridge: Cambridge University Press, 1995).

21 Przeworski *et al.*, *Sustainable Democracy*; and see also: Michael Margolis, *Viable Democracy* (Harmondsworth: Penguin Books, 1979).

22 For a summary of which see: R.H. McLeod and R. Garnaut, *East Asia in Crisis: From Being a Miracle to Needing One?* (London: Routledge, 1998); and R.J. Barry Jones, *The World Turned Upside Down? Globalization and the Future of the State* (Manchester: Manchester University Press, 2000), chapter 10.

Further reading

Brewer, A., *Marxist Theories of Imperialism* (London: Routledge & Kegan Paul, 1980). A most effective introduction to the Marxist approach to imperialism

Caporaso, James A., (ed.), *The Elusive State: International and Comparative Perspectives* (Newbury Park, CA: Sage, 1989). A wide-ranging review of the nature of the state and its effects.

Huntingdon, Samuel P., *The Clash of Civilizations and the Remaking of World Order* (New York: Simon & Schuster, 1996). A famous, almost notorious, think-piece on the cultural sources of major international conflicts in the future.

Penrose, Margaret, *Pathogenesis of War* (London: H.K. Lewis, 1963). A succinct review of the cultural and psychological sources of war.

Smith, Anthony D., *National Identity*, (Harmondsworth: Penguin Press, 1991). An authoritative review of the notions of nationality and nationalism.

Waltz, Kenneth, *Man, the State and War* (New York: Columbia University Press, 1959). The classic discussion of the varying sources of war in human affairs.

Woodcock, George, *Anarchism: A History of Libertarian Ideas and Movements* (Harmondsworth: Penguin Books, 1963). A wide-ranging and authoritative discussion of the whole range of anarchist and anti-statist political theory and practice.

4 International systems

Patterns

The international system

Theorists of international relations have striven long and hard to find an explanation for international behaviour, as has been seen. The ultimate goal of their study has not always been the creation of a permanent peace but rather the establishment of conditions of reasonable stability. The approach to this problem has been conducted at several different levels: that of the individual statesman, that of the individual state and that of the international system taken as a whole. This last view may be said to be reflected in the thinking of those theorists who advocate the concept of balance of power as the best means of ensuring equilibrium within the international system, if such a phenomenon might be said to exist. At the core of such thinking is the belief that it is a system[1] of formally sovereign states, operating in the absence of a single, central government, that constitutes the most important feature of international relations during the modern era. The assertion of this defining role for the system has led to the characterisation of the pattern of relations between states as being what one distinguished academic, Hedley Bull, has called an 'anarchic society':[2] a system that, despite the absence of a central power and authority, can nevertheless ensure peace and stability within its jurisdiction and the existence of shared principles of conduct that allow states to co-exist and inter-relate in a more or less orderly manner for much of the time. Whether individual states can act together in a coherent manner and help to create a system of international relations is thus a question that has become of central importance to the debate about the nature of modern international relations.

For the student of international relations, the idea that there might be such a thing as an international system is often seen as a complex and difficult concept to grasp. The nature of international

Balance of power – ambiguity and meaning

- The term balance of power may be used for:
  any distibution of power
  a particular distribution of power
- Balance of power may be:
  a policy or an outcome
- Geographically, balance of power may be:
  global or local
- Structurally, balance of power may be:
  simple or complex
  balanced or favourable imbalanced
- Analytically, balance of power may be:
  objective or subjective

Sources: Hedley Bull, *The Anarchical Society: A Study of Order in World Politics* (London: Macmillan, 1977) chapter 5 and others.

politics has sometimes been thought to be too disparate and too much involved with such a range of competing variables as to make any kind of systematic analysis inappropriate. Furthermore, those that attempt to use historical events as the basis on which to build an analysis of international behaviour are faced with the fact that many such events are unique in terms of the circumstances from which they arose. This leads to the conclusion that human beings are unlikely to be easily placed in neatly defined categories and that their behaviour is likely to be influenced by so many unknown factors that any analysis of past human behaviour is only an uncertain guide to likely future activity. Indeed, contemporary critical theorists argue that even to attempt to identify such regularities is to deny the central role of language and ideas in the creation of all human 'realities'.[3]

However, it is fair to note that throughout the history of relations between states, periods of war and peace have alternated with a high degree of regularity. The desire to reduce the deadly impact of war and to control events such that peace may become the norm rather than the exception has also been a factor that few commentators on international relations could readily ignore. Thus, despite the difficulties, the search for a means of managing relations between states in such a way that the incidence of war is greatly reduced has been a key issue that has dominated the thinking and writing about international relations in recent centuries.

> **An international (or inter-state) system**
>
> A regular and identificable pattern of significant interactions amongst relatively long-lived states

Some leading academics in the field of international politics, such as Kenneth Waltz,[4] have argued that the analysis of the nature and structure of the international system is central to an effective study of international relations, arguing that the structure of the system is a key factor in determining how the system operates as a whole and, consequently, how individual states behave within it. Such an analytical approach suggests that the structure of the system cannot be reduced to the characteristics of any one, or more, of its member states and that, in essence, it is to be regarded as a whole which is greater than the sum of its parts. Supporters of Waltz's approach thus argue that, as a consequence, it is imperative to study the nature and dynamics of international systems, past and present, which they believe is clearly essential if a proper understanding of international relations is to be achieved. Indeed, Kenneth Waltz explicitly sought to endow the analysis of the international system with the same kind of analytical, and even explanatory, power that he believed the analysis of market structure gave to economics.[5]

Neo-realism, as this approach has been termed to distinguish it from the more state-focused approach of classical Realism, involves the implicit claim, as Waltz's critics have pointed out, that the international system exists, in some sense, prior to the states of which it is composed.[6] Furthermore, such study can be focused upon the historical record of systems and/or the logical qualities of different kinds of systems. In recent years, both undertakings have occupied a number of the leading analysts of international relations.

The structural dynamics of modern international relations

It is generally agreed that the birth of the modern structure of international relations took place in 1648. In that year the Treaty of Westphalia was signed. This treaty brought to an end the Thirty Years War of Religion that had dominated Europe in the most recent past. The simple formula of directly relating the religion of the state to that of its ruler created the basis for the emergence of what was essentially a group of secular states in Europe. In the new order most, if not all, states subscribed to the principle of the 'Divine Right of Kings' as the basis for government.

Thus was established in 1648 a new structure which became known in the literature as the classical balance of power, the member states of which all shared a broadly similar ideology. In addition, the structure was dominated by a number of significant great powers – England, France, Prussia, Russia and Austria-Hungary – and came to be regarded as an example of a multi-polar balance. Given the ideological compatibility of the states concerned, it was clear that alliances could be formed between any of the leading players. Under this structural arrangement, alliances were not normally formed until wars were deemed to be likely to occur or in some cases had actually broken out. In consequence, alliances were seen as short-term arrangements often only lasting for the duration of that particular conflict, with the partners in the alliance free to choose alternative allies if another conflict broke out at a later date.

The Neo-Realist approach to the international system focuses upon the kind of distribution of power and capability of which the classical balance of power was one prime example. To a Neo-Realist, like Waltz, it was precisely the existence of five or so relatively well-matched powers that formed the basis of a classical balance of power system, with flexible alliance formation and the possibility of individual states acting as balancers. Indeed, Waltz contended in *The Theory of International Politics* that it was the switch from such a multi-power system to one dominated by just two superpowers after the Second World War that constituted the only real change of any significance in international politics throughout the modern period from 1648.

Change to such an international structure like the classical balance of power can come about in two ways. First, it is possible that the leaders of states could fail to act in ways that accord with the requirements of such a system[7] and thereby bring about developments that alter the number of significant powers within the system and/or the distribution of relative sources of strength and capability. Second, it is possible that the distribution of relevant capabilities will be altered by exogenous developments that are not directly addressed within Neo-Realism: economic developments, the exhaustion of resources or discovery of new sources, technological innovations, or, possibly, the introduction of racial military techniques.

The distributional changes that heralded the arrival of the bi-polar Cold War after the Second World War exemplify the kinds of developments that are highlighted in Walt's Neo-Realism. In contrast to the flexibility of the classical balance of power, the dominant bi-polar distribution of capability and power of the Cold War period generated a zero-sum approach to international politics. However, the bi-polar structure also simplified the situation, clarifying the responsibility that the two protagonists had for all major developments, including peace and war, and, with the added ingredient of nuclear weapons, shared control over the very lives of the greater part of mankind.

The character, dynamic and general implication of multi-polar systems – and the classical balance of power system in particular – and bi-polar systems are thus entirely different from a Neo-Realist point of view. Equally distinct would be a virtual global empire, or imperium, with one overwhelming power dominating the system, its other constituent parts and its ultimate development.

Neo-Realism – system characteristics

- Ordering principle (hierarchy/anarchy)
- Functions of different member units (leadership, etc.)
- Distribution of capabilities amongst units/states

Source: Keneth Waltz, *Theory of International Politics* (New York: Addison-Wesley, 1979), chapter 5.

One of the major weakness of Waltz's Neo-Realism, however, is its inability to address the immediate sources of such changes in critical capabilities and their international distribution, particularly when the past functioning of the system itself might have prompted some of those changes. It is this weakness that, in part at least, encouraged the development of a more refined derivative of Neo-Realism – the Structural Realism of Buzan, Jones and Little, with its accommodation of economic and ideological factors.[8]

Structural Realism acknowledges, in turn, some debt to the various forms of world systems theory, which seek to locate specific eras of international relations within the wider, and longer-term, patterns and processes of production and exchange on a world-wide basis.[9]

Many of the additional sources of the international system that has existed during the modern era, however, are precisely those features of 'modern' state and international politics that are highlighted by many critics of Waltz's Neo-Realism, who argue, as will be seen in the next chapter, that the nature and functioning of the state in the modern era have actually been the well-spring of the associated system of international relations: its nature, dynamic and effects.

Empirical patterns

The sources of the international system, and its characteristic structures, thus remain largely exogenous, or external to the factors and variables directly analysed, within Kenneth Waltz's Neo-Realism. The international systems that have existed throughout recent centuries are actually more complex than can be captured by Neo-Realism and many of the sources lie within the institutions that have arisen and come to define the 'modern' era, at least within the 'West'.

During the period of classical balance of power, such wars as did break out often reflected the *realpolitik* or power politics nature of the relations between the states and were largely concerned with dynastic issues of succession or territorial advantage rather than with ideological principles. The War of the Spanish Succession (1701–13), as its name implies, is but one clear example of this phenomenon. Furthermore, during much of the existence of the classical era of balance of power, wars were fought according to generally agreed rules of behaviour that were widely observed especially since it was the case that today's enemy could well be tomorrow's ally. Many of these rules were progressively codified within the growing body of international law.[10] In theory at least, alliances within this structure of states were capable of continuous readjustment depending on the circumstances prevailing at the time. However, it could be argued that a broad pattern of relationships did seem to emerge between the prominent members of the structure, although they were by no means permanent as the so-called 'Diplomatic Revolution' that took place in the mid-1750s demonstrated.[11] More often than not, the leading states in Europe divided evenly, although England, because of its island status and consequential emergence as a naval power, often sought to play the role of balancer within the structure. This role suited the English as it enabled their country to build the first of its Empires and retain not only an imperial role but also a strengthened economic status for a substantial number of years. The role of balancer was also recognised as ensuring that no one state, or group of states, became too powerful and gained a dominant position within Europe. Thus for much of the period after 1648 the primary purpose of the alliances that underlay the balance of power was less concerned with the destruction of the enemy as with the preservation of the structure, in general, and the leading members of it, in particular. Such patterns of shared norms and expectations formed the basis of what members of the 'English School' of international relations theory have termed an international society: a 'society', in some sense of the word, supposedly comprised of states, or at least their political elites and policy-makers.[12]

It is also important to point out that under these arrangements, when wars did occur between the alliance members in Europe, they were fought mainly for position rather than for outright and enduring victory. Although the outcome was important – why would anyone fight unless they believed that to be the case? – the final outcome was not regarded as likely to destroy the carefully balanced state structure. This again reflected the generally shared consensus on ideology and the willingness of opposing sides to agree peace terms, even if these sometimes meant that they had to sacrifice the interests of lesser members of the structure. The example of Poland, which was divided up on several occasions between the great powers in the eighteenth century, is a good illustration of this phenomenon. As far as the leading members of the structure were concerned, Poland was regarded as expendable and could, therefore, be used to offer territorial compensation to other, more important states whose favourable support was necessary in order to maintain the integrity of the existing *status quo*.

The only serious challenge to the classical balance of power came about as a result of the French Revolution and the wars that followed it. Napoleon unleashed a new ideological factor on the world, the concept of nationalism.[13] He mobilised what could be regarded as a citizen army and adopted a revolutionary approach to warfare. These new tactics upset the 'normal' way by which wars had previously been fought and the old 'rules of the game' were ignored in favour of highly effective if unorthodox methods of fighting. The heightened intensity of warfare both reflected and stimulated the process of military innovation. These innovations reflected a number of factors: the growing industrialisation of the age, improvements in transport and the perceived threat to the existing structure of European international relations. However, once Napoleon had been defeated at Waterloo, the victorious powers lost no time in attempting to restore the pre-Revolutionary status quo at the Congress of Vienna.

The restored structure of European international relations became known as the Concert of Europe. The new structure was arguably less violent than it predecessor, with the Crimean War being one of the few military disruptions to the diplomacy that was now more widely used in resolving dispute.

A further explanation for this relatively peaceful period in European history may have been the result of the fact that most European states in the meanwhile continued to industrialise and to embark on extensive colonial expansion. It might also have been regarded as the calm before the storm, because in Europe the greater part of the nineteenth century was also a period of development both in terms of new military technology and internal political change. For example, the unification of Italy and also of Germany demonstrated the fact that nationalism was still a powerful force. Growing urbanisation of the population in other states also increased the feelings of nationalism and the demands for political rights. These changes had a significant impact on the political relations between the leading states in Europe and, as the nineteenth century drew to a close, the great powers tended to drift towards more permanent alliance groupings, thus ending the earlier flexibility. The tendency of the system to become transformed, unofficially at least, into a bi-polar rather than a multi-polar structure resulted, according to some analysts, in the intensification of confrontation, the generation of 'arms races' and, ultimately, the outbreak of the First World War.[14] They also pointed to the role played by diplomats and the growing suspicion that the existence of secret treaties further inflamed the situation. On the other hand, radical theorists like Lenin argued that the scramble for economic advantage, and the colonialism that accompanied it had led to a 'crisis of capitalism' which could only end in cataclysmic war and the emergence of a new and better international order.[15]

The outbreak of the First World War in 1914 marked a return to ideological conflict and a form of warfare that engulfed a large number of states before becoming trapped in a protracted stalemate with neither side able to land a final and decisive blow. This came about, in part, because the war also saw the adoption of significantly different strategic objectives, such as the unconditional surrender of the opposing alliance. This change from the previous system of limited objectives reflected the emergence of the kind of total warfare that early military strategists like Karl von Clausewitz in his famous work, *On War*,[16] had suggested could become the case if wars ceased to be fought for limited political objectives. In part it could be said that it also reflected the increased involvement of large numbers of citizens in the fighting, particularly after the introduction of mass conscription. If the people of a state were to be forced to fight, they had to be given a cause to fight for. The portrayal of the enemy in entirely negative terms and the use of propaganda led to a further move away from the ideologically homogenous structure of the classical balance of power. The calls for the unconditional surrender of the enemy meant that compromise was impossible and the total humiliation of the defeated states was a necessary corollary. In consequence the peace settlement that followed the First World War was on punitive terms that were dictated to the vanquished states, whose interests and concerns were considered to be of little significance. The purpose of the new post-1919 international structure, albeit dressed up as a collective security system[17] designed to protect the interests of all, through a collective commitment to oppose acts of international aggression, became a thinly disguised attempt to ensure that Germany and its defeated allies were kept in a position of permanent inferiority in relation to those that had defeated them.

In addition to the increased levels of public participation seen during its course, the First World War also marked the start of a long period of considerable technological change with the introduction of tanks, submarines and aircraft into the armouries of most major states. The military value of aircraft became increasingly important. The idea of bombing enemy civilians in an effort to destroy both war-fighting capability and national morale became significant factors in war planning. This process of targeting what became regarded as value targets was taken to its logical conclusion during the Second World War and resulted in the destruction of many European cities and, ultimately, the use of the atomic bomb in Japan in August 1945.

Arguably the European structure of international relations could be said to have all but collapsed in 1914, but the defeat of Germany and the failure of the proposed alternative structures led to its reconstitution once again. The alternative centres of power – the United States and the Soviet Union – were excluded either because of the isolationist policy of the former or the ideological communist dogma of the latter. Furthermore the efforts to develop international institutions, such as the League of Nations, to control disputes between states, as well as efforts to proceed towards some degree of international disarmament, made little progress. As has been noted, the victorious states from the First World War adopted a punitive attitude to those that they had defeated and the League was seen as an instrument designed to reinforce the Versailles Treaty rather than to promote greater international understanding. However, as time went on, it became clear that neither Britain nor France possessed either the will or the capacity to enforce their wishes effectively. Although the new structure was designed to prevent the resurgence of Germany, it was equally vehemently opposed to the ideological threat that seemed to emanate from the Soviet Union. The leading states of the international system failed either to contain German recovery or to undermine the Soviet Union and once again the world was plunged into widespread chaos and instability.

The end of what became known as the Twenty Years' Crisis[18] was marked by the outbreak of the Second World War, by far the most ideological and destructive war fought for many centuries, if not of all time. At the end of this conflict the European structure, on which international relations had up until that time been based, lay in ruins and a new structure finally did emerge. This structure differed markedly from the previous one. It was essentially a bi-polar structure and the relationship between the two leading members of this new balance of power arrangement was described as the Cold War. The bi-polar structure that emerged consisted of alliances fixed around two major power centres: the United States and the Soviet Union. Membership of an alliance was generally determined by ideological factors and the existence of atomic weapons meant that the possibility of nuclear annihilation hung over all states. This led some commentators to describe the structure as less of a balance of power and more of a balance of terror, in which the Cold War protagonists deterred one another through the threat of mutual nuclear devastation. Unlike previous balance structures, the bi-polar structure relied less on the need to deter war by making it impossible for one side to win because each side was approximately in balance. Instead it relied on the deterrent factor of mutual assured destruction, which did not necessarily require a equal balance of resources. Furthermore, the more permanent nature of the alliances meant that greater planning and higher degrees of cooperation could be achieved, so that the alliance structures were more efficient and effective than those that had existed in previous structures.

Thus, the period of Cold War that followed after 1945 reflected to an even greater extent than previously, the 'security dilemma' that faces all states: the dilemma created by the fact that efforts to promote security unilaterally, through the acquisition of greater military capability, may all too readily prompt others to arm themselves in response to what they perceive to be the increased threat now coming from the security-seeking state. In the nuclear age, such a security dilemma represented a very serious challenge, as the arms race that accompanied the Cold War was concerned with qualitative as well as quantitative improvements in weaponry. Despite this, the structure remained comparatively stable. Although minor wars did take place and each side indulged in a fair degree of 'brinkmanship' – of taking confrontations to the verge of armed conflict with the other side, but (hopefully) not beyond – there was no direct confrontation involving the leading powers and their allies. Arguably this was mainly as a consequence of the rational leadership of the dominant powers and the strict adherence to the principles of nuclear deterrence, or, given the problematical character of 'rationality' on nuclear weaponry, the assertion of a higher, human rationality over the strict logic of military action and reaction. This stability was even visible in the process of change and accommodation that greeted the emergence of other nuclear states and the ultimate collapse of the ideological struggle that had dominated the Cold War.

Sources

Clearly, the issue of the status of the international system remains something of a problem. In one sense, the idea of 'the international system' may serve no purpose more serious than providing a linguistic shorthand for the complex actions and reactions in the 'international' sphere. If, on the other hand, the international system is supposed to have real effects upon the nature of international relations, then it is important to identify the possible sources of the system and its effects. The problem here is, as has already been suggested, to differentiate between the system, as such, and the characteristics of its member states – their guiding philosophies and the aspirations and expectations of their leaders.

As far as most traditional theorists of international relations are concerned what does appear to have remained as a constant basis for any international system has been the view that states are compelled to be self-regarding and to protect their own interests within an anarchical system, rather than to advance more globally defined interests: an interpretation which is complicated in the international society approach to international relations and which also may be changing, slowly, under the pressures of the post-Cold War world. To date, the hierarchical structure of the balance of power has meant that the key motivation of states at the top of any particular order has been the desire to stay at the top and to do all that was necessary to ensure that this remained the case. During the period of the Cold War, for example, it was clear that the superpowers operated within defined spheres of influence within which they were comparatively free to operate as they thought fit in resolving local difficulties. Thus, the United States was able to deal with Greece and Turkey when a dispute arose between them over Cyprus, and the Soviet Union was able to use military force to put down opposition in Hungary in 1956 and Czechoslovakia in 1968.

On the other hand, given the propensity of states to wish to expand and their ability to come into conflict with other states, it has generally been recognised by balance of power theorists that some mechanism for 'letting off steam' is absolutely essential. As already noted, in the nineteenth century this escape valve had been provided by the establishment of colonial empires around the globe that diverted European energies away from direct military involvement with each other.[19] Similarly, in the Cold War, the superpowers used every opportunity they could to exploit opportunities to engage in indirect conflicts with each other, almost always being careful to manage their affairs in such a way that direct 'hot' wars did not break out. Although this policy of brinkmanship sometimes went wrong, as over Cuba in 1962, it could generally be argued that during the bi-polar period of the Cold War rational decisions were made and the unwritten 'rules of the game' observed. The rules appeared to be that wars by proxy, or using surrogates, as occurred in the Middle East and Southern Africa were acceptable means of indirect conflict. Similarly, where one superpower was directly involved in a conflict, as in Vietnam or Afghanistan, the other superpower would only offer indirect support to its opponent's adversary.

The extent of indirect conflict during the Cold War became the basis for a further refinement of balance of power theory. One element of the bi-polar world that caused some discussion among academic observers was whether it should be regarded as 'tight' or 'loose'. A tight bi-polar system was defined as one in which all or almost all states would be absorbed into the sphere of influence of one or other of the superpowers; a loose bi-polar system was defined as one in which a significant number of states were not aligned to either superpower. Theorists like Karl Deutsch and J. David Singer[20] and Richard Rosecrance[21] have, in their differing ways, suggested that in an era of zero-sum thinking in which the gains of one side were offset by losses on the other, a tight bi-polar system might hold considerable danger of global conflict as every incursion could spark an uncontrollable war. Ironically, given their claim that by being non-aligned the neutralist states could help to resolve superpower disputes, it was precisely those Third World areas that remained outside the superpowers' spheres of influence that provided the 'safest' areas of conflict during the Cold War, whereas Europe, where the Cold War division was at its tightest, enjoyed a long peace.[22]

Problems

Analytical

Although the notions of an international system and the balance of power had played a dominant role in thinking about relations between states, both in theory and practice, there gradually developed a considerable body of academic criticism of traditional thinking about the concepts. Dating back to Greek times, the principles of the balance of power have been reported on and described by many writers on politics and diplomatic history. At the heart of this discussion is, as has been indicated, the belief that in an anarchical system, states either individually or in groups can only provide stability by accumulating military strength and/or by forming alliances and relationships that counter-balance each other. Some states may even be able to choose to remain neutral or play a role in maintaining stability by not committing themselves to either side until the last minute. Such structures have been observed over many different time periods and, whilst not excluding the possibility of war, have been seen by their supporters as being the best that can be hoped for in the relations between nations.

As has been made clear, the concept of balance of power has had a mixed press and it has been the subject of the highest praise and the greatest criticism. At one extreme it is possible that the simplest method of assuring peace was to create a genuine balance of power, by which they meant that power would be equally distributed between all states in the international community. At the other extreme there is the danger that an equal distribution of power, far from encouraging peace, could be a stimulant for war because a surprise attack by one side might be sufficient to tip the balance in its favour. Preponderant power might thus be the essential quality if an international structure is to be created in which peace could be properly ensured: a view which might encourage the conclusion that the only truly stable balance of power structure would be a uni-polar system in which one great power dominated all the rest. Finally, it is also possible that the secrecy that was created by the alliances that underpinned the balance of power structure was itself destabilising by inducing a heightened sense of insecurity and might have been one of the primary causes of the two great wars of the early part of the twentieth century. The wars of the European balance of power era might thus demonstrate the inherent instability and failure of the system to ensure either equilibrium or peace.

Thus, whilst the concept of the balance of power has been used frequently by academics and politicians and has been adapted to meet changing times, there is , as has been seen, considerable controversy over the precise nature of the concept of the balance of power. One possibility is that the term remains little more than empty rhetoric, while, to one influential commentator: 'the problem with balance of power is not that it has no meaning but that it has too many'.[23] The very versatility of the concept of balance of power suggests that the latter view is perhaps more accurate than the former.

Most academic writers on the subject of international relations have thus identified the concept of balance of power as having a significant range of different meanings. At one extreme, some analysts take the view that the balance of power is the result of an automatic process whereby the international system is always in balance; at the other extreme, there is a group of experts who take the view that it is only through the exercise of diplomatic skill that the international system remains in balance.[24] The former view implies that for every great power or group of powers that comes into existence the international balance will be preserved because another great power or group of powers will automatically arise to act as a counter-balance. In other words, within any given international structure there will always be some form of balance of power that operates come what may and that this is the natural and normal condition of relations between states. Conversely, it is possible that the process by which the balance of power is maintained is the result of painstaking diplomacy by world statesmen and is achieved by the careful construction of alliances and blocks of states. Thus, the balance of power may be seen as reflecting the perceived need for individual statesmen to play the central role in establishing effective and balanced structures on which international peace and security can be based. Finally, there is a compromise view that envisages that, although there is a general tendency for the system to be in balance, there is, nevertheless, a need for a balancer to give the process a helping hand and thus ensure the system remains stable. This final interpretation might be seen to place the emphasis on the role of an individual or identifiable state within the system whose purpose is to stand aloof from the system until required to support the weaker side in order to restore equilibrium. The fact that the concept of balance of power can be interpreted in so many different ways could arguably be said to support the Richard Cobden view that the concept is something that means all things to all men.

In addition, scholars of international relations have also sought to explain the intended purpose of balance of power within the context of four different interpretations.[25] First, the concept is seen to be a useful tool that can be used to describe the current distribution of power, either at a regional or at a global level. In this context the term balance of power can be seen to help with the establishment of the hierarchical order of states either on a global or a more local basis. Second, traditional theory of international politics interprets the concept of balance of power as referring to a policy which states desiring to retain the present distribution of power might usefully follow. This has led to the existence of a further interpretation of the concept as little more than propaganda to be used to defend the existing status quo against challengers who might seek a redistribution of power, which in turn would upset the balance and cause disruption. Finally, some more recent work by international relations analysts has attempted to characterise balance of power as a system.[26]

The first interpretation of balance of power as a descriptive tool is easily considered. The hierarchy of states would recognise the existence, especially in recent times, of superpowers which might possess such power as to be able to defeat any opponent, including another superpower; great powers which have global interests and global capabilities and which until recently were seen as being at the top of the international hierarchy, medium powers which have regional interests and regional capabilities, and, at the bottom of the list, small powers which have limited resources and very limited interests. Each level of the hierarchy, except those at the very top, may find themselves the victims of those above them in the structure. The term is simply used to describe any existing distribution of power without ascribing any moral value to it. Thus, commentators may state that 'the balance of power is shifting' when they mean that the current balance has been changed in favour of one alliance or party or another. On the other hand, simply describing a states hierarchical position in relation to others may not give a full picture, as the power of one state may not be as appropriate as that of a state perceived to be far weaker. For example, the United States, clearly a superpower, failed to win the war in Vietnam in part because the basis of their superpower status was inappropriate to the task they had to undertake; similarly, Britain and France, both great powers, failed to defeat the clearly militarily inferior Egyptians during the Suez Crisis of 1956 because of external pressures. It might also be added that the simplistic approach to power is further misleading in two further ways. First, states might be regionally important great powers but play little or no role on the global stage, the example of South Africa during the apartheid years might be a good illustration of this phenomenon. Second, there appears to be an implicit assumption that once a state achieves the status of being a great power it remains so, but this is clearly not the case as states' relative and absolute power relations are constantly in flux.

Much more prominent in the literature, however, is the second interpretation that regards balance of power as a foreign policy strategy. This approach has been adopted by many traditional writers on international relations who argue that balance of power is likely to be pursued as a policy by those that wish to achieve and maintain stability in the relations between members of the international community.[27] However, some states have sought to argue that, in order for stability and equilibrium to occur, it is necessary for either themselves and/or their allies to be slightly stronger than their potential opponents. In this sense the concept of balance of power is more akin to a bank balance where outgoings and incomings rarely, if ever, are equal rather than to a scale balance where equal weights always balance. It should be made clear that the former concept of the bank balance analogy does not equate an equilibrium balance with an even distribution of power. Rather it suggests that international stability is created by being stronger than an opponent so as to ensure that the other side will not attempt to upset the balance. On the other hand, there were those states and international relations scholars who have argued that, in order for there to be peace and stability, power ought to be evenly distributed within the system so that no one state could win a war and thus no rational state would start a war. In other words, the scales on a fulcrum analogy support the belief that stability can be achieved if the structure is in perfect balance because balanced power is negated power and states will not, therefore, fight. It is important that students attempt to distinguish clearly between 'equilibrium' meaning stability and the term 'equal distribution of power'.

The view that power ought to be evenly distributed if stability is to be achieved encounters significant difficulties. Acceptance of such an even distribution is essentially idealistic; most states would, in practice, prefer a 'cushion of security', through knowing that they, rather than their opponents, are slightly the stronger party if there is any possibility whatsoever of future conflict. As a consequence of the perceived need to be slightly stronger than the opposing side, states pursuing a policy of balance of power have frequently engaged in arms races. This has certainly been a feature of several different kinds of balance system whether it was multi-polar, as was the case in the eighteenth and nineteenth centuries, or it was bi-polar, as was the case during the post-1945 Cold War: a 'war' that was 'fought' between the Union of Soviet Socialist Republics and its affiliates and the United States of America and its allies but without the direct use of armed force between the major protagonists. Thus, far from advocating a process by which power would be equally balanced, most Realist advocates of the balance of power regarded it as a desirable foreign policy objective, that states should invariably seek to ensure that they were always more powerful than their opponents, since failure to do so would lead to the collapse of the system and thence to chaos and war.

It is possible that arms races increase instability, particularly if they are conducted on the basis of quantity rather than quality.[28] Whilst there need never be an end to quality – every weapon can always be improved upon – the question of 'how much is enough?' is one that may be asked if the race is numerical. Instability is made worse by the fact that a state that is falling behind in the race might feel that it needs to fight before it is too late and its opponent is too far ahead; conversely, states that are far ahead may relax too much and allow their opponents to catch up or even overtake them. These arguments are ones that were familiar in the language of the Cold War, with politicians and their supporters in the military talking in the United States of the 'missile gap' and the 'window of vulnerability'.

The concept of balance of power may also be no more that a propaganda tool to defend the current distribution of power and to protect the interests of those states that currently exercise the greatest influence within the international structure of the day. This last point has brought home to many observers the fact that one of the key purposes of balance of power has been primarily designed to preserve the interests and continued existence of the few great powers, even at the expense of the survival and interests of the many, lesser powers. Under this arrangement lesser states could and would be sacrificed partially or wholly for the satisfaction of the needs of the leading members of the balance of power structure. The example of the fate of Poland in the eighteenth century is a good illustration of the treatment handed out to those states regarded as being of little importance to the survival of the structure as a whole and, therefore, expendable. Nevertheless, by appealing to the idea that any redistribution of power might lead to chaos and destruction, balance of power consequently became a powerful ideological tool for conservative forces to use in arguing against demands for reform and in presenting the case for the preservation of the structure of state relations in its current form. It was certainly indicative of the basic analysis that states were essentially self-interested and acted out of motives that reflected their own specific interests rather than general international interests. Thus it could be asserted that, for those at the apex of the hierarchy of states, pursuit of balance of power appealed to their selfish interests.

On the other hand, this conservative approach meant that those states that were dissatisfied with their power position were placed in the unenviable position of either having to choose to accept their lot or of having to fight to improve it. This became a central issue of concern over the value of balance of power as a means of managing international relations and of maintaining equilibrium. Whilst it has been shown that the very imprecise nature of its definition makes it a flexible policy, there still remains the central question of how, in the dynamic world of international politics, a concept that is so rooted in maintaining an inflexible status quo can accommodate and adjust to change.

As the so-called behavioural revolution advanced during the 1960s, two distinct lines of response to the 'traditional' study of international relations emerged: one, as will be seen later, which simply denied the empirical reality, and theoretical utility, of the idea of an international system;[29] the other which criticised what 'traditional' analysts saw as its main strength: the imprecise nature of conceptions of the international system and definitions of such central concepts as the balance of power.[30] The attack on traditional international relations thinking led to one of the great controversies in international relations theory in recent years. As a result of this debate there emerged a group of theorists, spearheaded by Morton Kaplan,[31] who argued for a more scientific analysis of the subject matter of international politics. Among other issues this group argued in favour of greater precision in terms of definition of the key concepts used within the discipline. They also advocated less reliance on intuitive reasoning and argued that judgements based on sound empirical evidence would be a more appropriate method of reaching conclusions about international political behaviour. The exchange of views between this group and its opponents among the more traditional thinkers on the subject was often vitriolic and led, for a time, to a clear division within the discipline.

Morton Kaplan's approach to the subject matter of international politics was not to reject the idea that balance of power was a useful concept in analysing the behaviour of states in international relations, but what he sought to do was to bring more clarity to the meaning of the concept. He sought to adopt a systems analysis approach to international politics and to treat relations between states as if they were operating within a system. States thus remained key variables within the system but operating in such a way as to preserve or destroy the existing structure.

Kaplan was thus able to identify what he saw as a number of variants on the theme of different potential 'balance of power' systems.[32] For each of these possible variants – balance of power; loose bi-polar; tight bi-polar; universal,[33] hierarchical[34] and unit veto[35] – Kaplan defined what he saw as the essential rules of each system.[36] If states ignored the essential rules of the system then, Kaplan argued, the system would fall into chaos and conflict. This was the means by which, according to this analysis, one system of balance of power would eventually be replaced by another one either of the same type but with different main players or, in more radical scenarios, by an entirely different structure altogether. Such an analysis highlights one of the central problems of ideas about the 'balance of power': whether it is to be viewed as an automatic, and possibly unintended, consequence of other developments, or whether it has to be the result of the conscious intentions and calculations of the leaders of those states that are to form a 'balance'. The complexity of this issue is illustrated by Kaplan's view that war is the specific catalyst of change and that if states did not wish to see changes taking place then they had to follow the identifiable 'essential rules' of the system: a complex mixture of the automatic and the intentional in the maintenance of a balance of power system, or, indeed, any other identifiable international system.

Using his model, Kaplan attempted to show how the traditional European-based multi-polar system had collapsed during the first half of the twentieth century because the key actors had failed, in his opinion, to maintain the essential rules. The Second World War had, thus, enabled the emergence of a radically different system, a bi-polar relationship between two superpowers who were effectively non-European states. However, it has to be recognised that this was made even more complex because of the existence of nuclear weapons, which meant that the new patterns of international behaviour had to be more restrained than in the past if the system, and indeed the world, was to survive.

Kaplan's approach created difficulties of its own, however. Critics of his attempt to establish that there is a workable system of balance of power have argued that the 'essential rules' he identified in the models were, in the main, all based on previous experience and had been adduced from analysis of either past or present behaviour.[37] Potentially, therefore, the 'essential rules' were basically historical descriptions, which offered little of value for predicting the future or in helping to formulate policy guidelines for the future. Second, in more pragmatic terms, the argument that war was the basis for change was unsustainable in the nuclear age and, as events have shown, the collapse of bi-polarity came about not as a result of conflict but through the exhaustion of one of the key players, who could no longer maintain its part in the confrontation. Thus, internal collapse rather than a great military conflict created the conditions that led to the end of the Cold War.

Such problems lent support to the alternative approach, developed by Richard Rosecrance, to categorise the European international system between 1740 and 1960 into nine 'systems' classified in terms of four critical factors or variables: disturbance elements (ideologies, domestic upheavals, etc.); the prevalent mechanism for regulating the system (war, 'concerts' of the larger powers, etc.); the environmental restraints; and, finally, the patterns of outcomes generated within the system. The nine distinct systems fell into one of the two groups of stable and unstable.[38]

Rosecrance's nine international systems

- Eighteenth Century (1740–89) (stable)
- Revolutionary Imperium (1789–1814) (unstable)
- Concert of Europe (1814–22) (stable)
- Truncated Concert (1822–48) (stable)
- Shattered Concert (1848–71) (unstable)
- Bismarkian Concert (1871–90) (stable)
- Imperialist Nationalism (1890–1918) (unstable)
- Totalitariam Militarism (1918–45) (unstable)
- Postwar (1945–60) (stable)

Rosecrance's four critical factors/variables for classifying international systems

- Disturbance elements – ideologies, domestic changes
- Regulative mechanisms (war, 'concerts' of big-power)
- Environmental restraints (resource limitations, etc.)
- Characteristic outcomes (wars, negotiated agreements, etc.)

Source: Richard Rosecrance, *Action and Reaction in World Politics* (Boston, MA: Little, Brown, 1963)

Other analysts, such as those who advocated the more complex, multi-level and multi-element, chandelier model of balance of power[39] argued that the structure was capable of adaptation without war, given its greater capacity to absorb a range of alterations of relative power in different areas of interest and/or geographical locations without plunging the entire system into disaster. For example, they pointed out that it had, in any case, changed from a bi-polar one and was already moving towards a tri-polar or even a multi-polar structure long before the end of the Cold War was finally signalled. First, the 1970s thus saw the emergence of the People's Republic of China as a putative superpower had been recognised both by academics and practising politicians. Thus the American policy of détente in the early years of the 1970s was designed to accommodate this phenomenon and to use it to the advantage of American interests and at the expense of those of the Soviet Union. Although at that time it was recognised that the Chinese lacked the economic power to sustain their growing military potential, nevertheless they posed a significant threat for the future. Second, the world had seen the emergence of Japan as a significant force in the international economy, even though, for obvious reasons, its military capability was severely restricted. Finally, the recovery of Europe had resulted in the emergence of the then European Community (now European Union) as a potential superpower with a sound military and economic base. In face of these developments, analysts began to consider how the change from a bi-polar system to a multi-polar system might be managed. Under the rigid system, formalised in Kaplan's models, there seemed to be little room for manoeuvre because of the strong hierarchical nature of the structure. An alternative view was to see the system in terms of clusters of states that were at once in balance with each other and balanced between each cluster. This raised again the question of whether a global system of balance of power could ever operate or whether a series of interlinked regional or local systems would form the basis of a future model for international stability.

Finally, an increasingly well-established body of writing emphasises the role of an international hegemon – a leading state with widespread influence, such as Great Britain in the nineteenth century or the United States of America since 1945 – on the shaping of the overall direction of development of an international sytem: exercising a decisive influence over political and military conflict; promoting new forms of economic organisation and/or production; and playing a leading role in the development and propagation of the dominant intellectual currents.[40]

Empirical

Even during the period when the classical balance of power structure was in existence, wars continued to take place. This could be interpreted as meaning that the interests of individual states had taken precedence over the interests of the international community as a whole. On the other hand, the nature of warfare in the years after 1648 was far less devastating or brutal than the ideologically based wars of religion that had preceded this period. Wars were largely fought for dynastic reasons and designed to prevent one or another of the great powers from becoming too powerful and thus a threat to the overall stability of the structure. In addition, during this time, wars were of comparatively short duration, they involved relatively low casualties and, for much of the period, with the exception of the Napoleonic wars, were fought by mercenary armies. Thus, the involvement of ordinary citizens in the wars of this period was relatively slight. This factor was also a reflection of a general agreement on tactics to be adopted during conflicts and on the weapons that were available to the military of the warring parties. It was generally the case that the military fought wars only during the good weather of the spring and summer months and according to set rules and procedures. These rules and procedures laid down how sieges were to be conducted and how prisoners and civilians were to be treated. Provided the rules were observed, wars were conducted in an orderly manner.

For much of the period also there was general agreement over the need for alliances which were relatively stable but, unlike their counterparts in the nuclear age, not permanent. Nevertheless, loyalties were quite strong and those states outside the immediate central actors were considered as being of little or no consequence. The concerns of the structure were centred on Europe rather than the wider world; indeed, the expansion of Empire and imperial conquest during this period testifies to the attitude adopted towards those not of immediate concern to the great powers.

Despite the problem of the Napoleonic period, which brought an albeit temporary ideological element to the conflict and thus greatly disturbed the stability of the structure, it was not until the industrial revolution had been fully felt that great advances were made in military science and technology. One of the side effects of the industrialisation of the period was to make citizens more aware of their nationality and loyalties and thus the age of nationalism came into existence. From this grew the inevitable consequence of creating difference between peoples and states that further intensified the political antagonisms between them. Alliances became increasingly more permanent and, whilst cooperation between alliance members increased, cooperation between members of different alliance structures became increasingly difficult. These changes meant that warfare became more intense and involved an ever-growing number of citizens, culminating in the establishment of the bi-polar Cold War structures after 1945.

The near rigidity of the post-1945 structure with its permanent alliances and the ever-present threat of nuclear destruction made international cooperation far more complex. The international system grew in size dramatically with the de-colonisation of most West European empires. However, the bi-polar structure seemed to prevent cooperation on all but the most minimal of levels within the global community. Thus, cooperation on such things as the eradication of disease or the resettlement of refugees was attempted but ideological differences meant that efforts to tackle international poverty and famine and environmental problems had to be left largely to the efforts of non-governmental organisations. It was only at the highest strategic level in the form of the desire not to destroy each other with accidental nuclear annihilation that the two superpowers found much broad measure of agreement.

It may be concluded that the very supposition of the theorists of balance of power that states have to protect their own position and power rather than act in accordance with a general view of the mutual benefits of global cooperation has substantial support from the long history of modern international relations. However, the ending of the Cold War must then be interpreted exclusively as a result of the Soviet Union's practical inability, for internal reasons, to sustain itself in a power game against the United States of America and her allies and exclude the possibility of a recognition of the intrinsic futility of the sustained and inherently dangerous confrontation between the two superpowers. Balance of power also encounters difficulties in dealing with critical developments like the decision of Great Britain not to make a power-preserving deal with Hitler's Germany in 1940 and to continue with the long and highly costly struggle to contain and finally defeat Nazism. Simple balance of power doctrines make problematical assumptions that international developments are driven either exclusively by the self-interest of those who have the capacity to influence external developments or by more complex (and possibility wishful) translation of self-protective behaviour into a contribution to the general, international good (through the preservation of the 'home of democracy' or the 'socialist motherland').

Solutions

The analytical and practical problems posed by the notion of the international system and the central concept of the balance of power are intertwined, as are the possible paths to their solution.

The analytical problems posed by the existence and nature of the international system, itself, have prompted a variety of responses. The rejection of the very notion of the system by Snyder, Bruck and Sapin[41] from within the behavioural tradition, has been continued by post-modernist and post-rationalist adherents to a quite different intellectual tradition. Efforts to produce richer and, hence, more illuminating analyses of the international system have also continued in the work of structural realists,[42] students of the dynamics of historical systems[43] and behavioural students of international system dynamics.[44]

At the interface between theoretical issues and practical concerns, some of the proposed solutions to the problem of war have reflected ideas that reflect the views of the 'Idealistic' school of international relations thinking. Such idealism was popular during the decades after the ending of the First World War, became highly influential within intellectual and academic circles and exercised considerable influence upon such innovations as the formation of the League of Nations.[45] The establishment of a system of collective security, in which all states would pledge themselves to come to the aid of any fellow state that fell prey to aggression from any other state(s), was the mechanism advocated for the solution of the perennial problems of conflict and insecurity.

Similar aspirations and expectations, to those that guided the creators of the inter-war international institutions, also motivate those who advocate the establishment of a world society and the contention that it is the state itself that is the problem and not the solution to the problem of how to avoid international conflict and war. According to this view, a world in which the state was subordinated, if not eliminated, and the accompanying establishment of a world society would develop a far more complex set of relationships that would bind individuals together in a web of interconnected interests. This approach, therefore, seeks to place the common interests of each individual or group at the general global level above loyalty to a particular state.[46]

The difficulties that confronted the attempts to achieve a working collective security system in the inter-war years and the post-Second

World War era, and the spectacular failure of the League of Nations in the face of Italian, Japanese and German aggression, have all been salutary, however. Genuine systems of collective security proved particularly difficult, not least because of the problem of getting anyone to join a structure that had to be taken on trust. Alliances could be seen as reliable because members would know who their friends were and in what precise circumstances they could expect assistance. On the other hand, in a collective security system everyone was the ally of everyone else but the guarantees were rather too vague and generalised. The fear has been that many states would expect others to support a fellow-member that got into trouble because they were nearer or stronger and, in consequence, a victim state might end up not getting any help at all. The only answer to this problem was that a working collective security system would require states to act in such a way that all freedom of choice would be removed. In such a scenario, states would all have to act in prescribed ways, either to settle dispute peacefully or, if that failed, to act against a state that was identified as the 'guilty party' regardless of their own individual view of the relative merits of the case. It might well be argued that if such a system could be established it could well be unnecessary because far from being a half-way house to world government, it would indeed have become a system of world government. Such a solution would result in the destruction of the autonomy of the state in international relations and the ultimate triumph of those who espoused the idealist view of relations between states.[47]

One response to the problem of potential rigidity and resistance to change in a balance of power system lies in exploring how states wishing to maintain the status quo ought to behave; another is to explore the extent to which it is possible that a rigid hierarchical system could be replaced by a view of inter-state relationships as being more closely defined by the model of a chandelier.

The chandelier model of balance of power[48] suggests that each 'level' of power relationships could be kept in balance and that any changes could be accommodated by a process of adjustment of the relationship between each member at a particular level. In other words, just as it is possible to increase the number of candleholders at each different level of a chandelier without upsetting its overall balance, so the balance of power could expand to accommodate new or more powerful members at each level within its structure. For example, the United States adopted a policy of détente in respect of both the Soviet

Union and the People's Republic of China in the 1970s once it recognised that the latter state was beginning to play a significant world role and in consequence the world structure was becoming tri-polar rather than a bi-polar. A further advantage, however, was that even the chandelier model retained the essential point that states should act in such a manner that would reflect their own self-interest.

The idea that states would only act in their own self-interest also, incidentally, put paid to the notion that some states might play the role of balancer in an unselfish way. Those states, like Great Britain in the nineteenth century, which claimed to be willing to play such a role did so because their interests were served by such a policy not out of altruism. Thus, for Britain in the nineteenth century, stability in Europe was an essential pre-requisite for an outward-looking and expansionist policy with regard to the development of trade and imperial conquest. In other words, Britain's imperialist ambitions were served by playing the balancer in Europe in order to add decisive strength to the weaker side of the balance and ensuring that, in consequence, no single state came to dominate the continent of Europe. Additionally, this British policy allowed for the expansion of its Empire even wider and for still further development of its economic prowess. Arguably, the 'scramble for Empire' also allowed a safety valve for the natural expansionist ambitions of states and diverted their attention, at least for a short while, away from fighting each other. However, it is possible that one of the root causes of the First World War lay in the frustrated imperial ambitions of some of the states who started too late in the race to gain colonies as much as in the economic rivalry that arose from the desire to gain overseas' markets.

In concluding this discussion it should be made clear that, despite its popularity as a term in both the vocabulary of politicians and international relations literature, the question of the meaning of the concept of balance of power is still one that is clouded in confusion.

It has already been argued that the term 'balance' is ambiguous and can be interpreted in a variety of ways, but this is as nothing when compared to the ambiguities that surround the concept of 'power'. It is clear that much of the traditional literature on balance of power concerns itself almost exclusively with military power as the major factor in determining relations between states and even then only really with those elements of military capability that can be measured. Such a view is both incomplete and often inaccurate as such immeasurable factors as the quality of leadership, morale of the armed forces, effectiveness of training, the sophistication and appropriateness of weaponry and degree of commitment to a particular cause cannot easily be judged but they each contribute markedly to the effectiveness of a state's international performance. As previously hinted, a simple measure of 'power' would not have persuaded any sensible person that the North Vietnamese would have been able to prevent the United States from winning in Vietnam nor that the rebels in Afghanistan would have been able to withstand the might of the Soviet Union. Similarly a simplistic assessment of the numerical relationship between Israel and its Arab neighbours would give little hint that the former had won four important military victories over the latter. Thus, even at its most simplistic, the idea of measuring power, in order to balance it, is fraught with difficulties and reinforces the point that power is relative and has a psychological aspect to it. This would be bad enough but, in modern international relations, the concept of power is concerned as much with economic, diplomatic and political factors as it is with military power, if not more so.

Whilst it might have been true that during the era of the classical balance of power the great powers of the day were also those that dominated all the other spheres of power mentioned above, this is certainly not the case today. States like Germany and Japan, both of whose military power has been greatly circumscribed until recently, are significant economic powers in contemporary international relations. Similarly, oil-rich states may possess considerable wealth but they lack status in other aspects of power. Furthermore, historical factors may influence the international reputation and external perception of some states who may retain a far greater influence and even authority over other states than their power status would currently support. In addition, states that are regarded as having had a long period of 'success' are generally likely to achieve more effective outcomes in foreign policy than those states perceived as having had an unsuccessful past. The position of Great Britain in contemporary world politics is a very clear example of this phenomenon. Britain has continued to wield influence far above that warranted by its physical capabilities and in recent years it has continued, as the former Foreign Secretary Douglas Hurd succinctly put it, 'to punch above its weight'. Similarly, individual leaders or the holders of particular internationally recognised offices may exert considerable influence over the behaviour of others which is far in excess of either their own or their home state's or authority's capability. The influence that Ayatollah

Khomenei had over the growth of Islamic fundamentalist views, the high international regard for the Papacy, not just in the spiritual but also from time to time in the political sphere, and the general respect and importance accorded to the holder of the office of UN Secretary General are cases in point.

It would, therefore not be unreasonable to conclude that, in contemporary international relations, the close correlation between power in a number of fields that could be said to have existed between the leading members of the eighteenth- and nineteenth-century balance of power structure and their great power status has been far less discernible among the great and superpowers that occupied centre stage during the latter half of the twentieth century. For example, during the bi-polar Cold War period, it would be difficult to portray the Soviet Union as ever having had the status of being a great economic power, with commensurate influence upon the functioning of the international economy. In recent decades, therefore, the nature of inter-state power relations has in consequence become far more complex than in previous centuries. This has been due not only to the fact that the number of states has vastly increased since the end of the Second World War but also to the fact the distribution and greater diffusion of the forms of power have created disparate hierarchies of states that clearly have not always overlapped in membership.

Prospects

Attempts to identify the existence of an international system as such have been fraught with difficulties and emphasising a model of the balance of power has been much criticised. As international relations moves into the post-Cold War period, a case can be made both for and against the continued existence of such a model of international relations. The dramatic collapse of the Soviet Union left the United States as the only superpower capable of taking a leading role in world affairs. This, arguably, at one level reflects the existence of a uni-polar system in which the United States plays the dominant and decisive role. However, the cost of its victory in the Cold War has meant that the USA has been very reluctant to carry the responsibility of world policeman alone and has sought partners around the globe either to offer financial or material support for any peace-keeping or peace-enforcing activities. Therefore, the current situation also reflects the weakness of a uni-polar system in so far as it is clear that the United

States is not interested in every dispute around the globe and will choose those that it wishes to get involved in according to its own perceived self-interest. The outlook for those that are ignored is poor as there does not seem to be enough effective power among other states to enforce a settlement. The demands for peace-keeping forces from the UN has not been met with a sufficient supply of forces or finance from states willing to undertake the different and difficult tasks that such exercises require. The much heralded 'new world order' proved to be rather less well ordered than was hoped. Many of the disputes that had been controlled during the Cold War became far more active, and inter- as well intra-state strife has increased enormously since the end of the 1980s. Whatever system might now be in place, if indeed there is one at all, few states have a very clear idea of what the main rules of the system are or how they should be applied.

Second, the end of the Cold War produced a new agenda of international relations. There are a number of reasons to believe that the old approach to the international system, based as it was on balance of power thinking and with it the emphasis upon the role of the state, may no longer be quite as valid as in the past. Thus in the most recent past, concern has been expressed that there should be a more collective and less selective response to international problems. This has brought with it a far greater emphasis on the UN as a centre for determining the international responses to crises than in the past. However, the UN has not fully lived up to expectations and changes will need to be brought about in its organisation and structure if its true potential is to be achieved. Some analysts welcomed the response of the UN to the Iraqi invasion of Kuwait in 1990 because it appeared to reflect a more collective response to an international crisis and not one that reflected merely Cold War intrigues. The near-unanimous condemnation of Iraq and the willingness of the international community to rally behind Kuwait seemed to suggest a basis for broad agreement on some basic rules of acceptable international behaviour. Rather more cynically, it can be pointed out that Kuwait was an oil rich state in which many leading members of the international community had a considerable financial and economic interest. Indeed, it is possible that the new role proposed for the UN has become a thinly disguised pax Americana in which US interests are the main driving force in determining whether or not the UN acts effectively. The proof of whether there really was a change of heart and a new world order would be found if and when the UN was able to act in a dispute which did not reflect these particular interests. The case of Bosnia and the failure of attempts to reach a political settlement prior to the involvement of President Clinton is a good example of the difficulties facing UN peace-keeping efforts, unless there is a clear understanding that its mandate will be enforced by overwhelming military capability if necessary.

Another post-Cold War trend has been away from the emphasis on individual states towards regional organisations. One consequence of the collapse of the Warsaw Pact as one side of the bi-polar European-centred international system has been to give its former rival, NATO, a new lease of life, playing the role of international peace-keeper for the UN and extending its membership to include some of its former opponents. In recent years attempts have been made to develop closer relationships within Europe by attempting to establish a framework for a common security and defence identity as well as a Permanent Joint Council with Russia. Three states – Poland, Hungary and the Czech Republic – have been invited to join NATO as full members and the prospect of further enlargement remains, at least in theory, open. All other European states outside NATO have been invited to join the Partnership for Peace (PfP), through which individual programmes of support and cooperation have been developed. There has also been the establishment of the Combined Joint Task Force (CJTF) to trouble shoot around the globe and which is made up out of contributions from NATO and PfP members. Thus, the NATO-led operation in Bosnia has had contingents from Partnership countries, including Russia and from states outside Europe, such as Morocco as well as NATO members. Finally, and perhaps most interestingly, NATO has begun a dialogue with what it calls the Mediterranean group which consists of Mauritania, Morocco, Tunisia, Egypt, Israel and Jordan. This suggests that NATO at least is beginning to consider the need to extend security beyond the sharply defined geographical boundaries of Cold War Europe.

Progress has been made in the creation of a European Union which would bind together existing members ever more closely in an economic and political arrangement. Like NATO, the EU has also been faced with the dilemma of how to deal with the expectations and aspirations of the emerging democracies of Eastern and Central Europe. Only time will tell whether this challenge will be effectively met, but what is clear is that the challenges to traditional ideas concerning state sovereignty are mounting and alternative methods of avoiding war between states are being developed which emphasise cooperation rather than confrontation.

A final challenge to traditional state centric systems theory as embodied in the balance of power comes from the idea of globalisation,[49] as will be seen in Chapter 5. During the twentieth century, war became increasingly globalised. As the First and Second World Wars clearly showed, there were few places that could escape the consequences of conflict and, as weapons of mass destruction became not only more widely available but more lethal, the consequences of significant warfare were too much to contemplate. The idea that there might be some future balance of power arrangement that would satisfy the varying needs of all the members of the international community seems equally unlikely. The possibility of a uni-polar world which arguably might have been contemplated had the United States taken up the reins of power after the end of the Cold War has now receded. In any case even the new world order that President Bush proposed would have been hard to imagine in reality and a system that failed to address the genuine grievances of the small and developing states in an adequate manner would merely be storing up trouble for the future. Public opinion may well be sympathetic to the plight of the suffering and the widespread support for charities operating in this area is proof of this. Similarly the support for humanitarian aid in civil wars and public horror at mass killings and ethnic cleansing suggests that television images are doing much to bring people closer together.

However, the translation of this sympathy into state action is more complex. Often the same people who argue that something ought to be done are the ones who expect that military action will be short, sharp and decisive and lead to a quick victory with low casualty rates for their own side. What was abundantly clear was that fighting a war in the desert against Iraq, even though it might have been far most costly than it eventually proved, was more attractive to many people than a long drawn out conflict in the inhospitable terrain of Bosnia.

Traditionally, balance of power systems have reflected the values and principles of the dominant states within them and these principles have rarely been shared by all – maybe not even by a majority – of the states in the international community. As a consequence, the idea that all states would have an interest in the existing status quo has always been unrealistic especially as the benefits of the system often applied only to a small group of favoured members who existed at or near the top of the international hierarchy. However, globalisation should have brought with it the realisation that all states have a vested interest in resolving common problems that threaten the existence of the planet. This wider agenda has broadened the basis on which states may seek relationships with others, although it might be argued that these are best resolved at a regional rather than a global level. Arguably, such regional arrangements could have overlapping memberships which would create a series of interconnected structures that would form a loose global structure. Such a view might not be as farfetched as it might seem if the NATO Mediterranean group was to be seen as a forerunner for what could be achieved. However, what is clear is that the realisation of such a long-term objective has yet to translated into an effective means of managing relations between members of the international community, the majority of whom continue to place their own interests ahead of the general interests of the community as whole. Until states are able to recognise the need to come together to harmonise their interests, students may still wish to argue that the idea of an international system of states is an academic ideal but not a concrete reality.

Notes

1 A system consisting of any regular pattern of significant interactions amongst identifiable parts (or actors) that persist through a sufficient period of time: the criteria of significance for interactions and sufficiency for time being, themselves, problematical matters.

2 Hedley Bull, *The Anarchical Society: A Study of Order in World Politics* (London: Macmillan, 1977).

3 For a survey of such views see: Jim George, *Discourses of Global Politics: A Critical (Re)Introduction to International Relations* (Denver, CO: Lynne Rienner, 1994).

4 Kenneth N. Waltz, *Theory of International Politics* (Reading, MA: Addison-Wesley, 1979).

5 Waltz, *Theory of International Politics*, pp. 89–91.

6 R.O. Keohane (ed.), *Neorealism and its Critics* (New York: Columbia University Press, 1986), especially the contribution by Richard K. Ashley, 'The poverty of neorealism', pp. 255–300.

7 Of the type formulated by Morton Kaplan in his pioneering, *System and Process in International Politics* (New York: J. Wiley, 1964).

8 B. Buzan, C. Jones and R. Little, *The Logic of Anarchy: Neo-Realism to Structural Realism* (New York: Columbia University Press, 1993).

9 For example: Immanuel Wallerstein, *The Modern World System, Vol. I: Capitalist*

Agriculture and the Origins of the European World-Economy in the Sixteenth Century (New York: Academic Press, 1974) and *The Modern World System, Vol. II: Mercantilism and the Consolidation of the European World-Economy, 1600–1750* (New York: Academic Press, 1980); A.G. Frank and B. Gills (eds), *The World System: Five Hundred Years or Five Thousand* (London: Routledge, 1993); and C. Chase-Dunn and T.D. Hall, *Rise and Demise: Comparing World Systems* (Boulder, CO: Westview Press, 1997).

10 Bull, *The Anarchical Society*, chapter 6.

11 On which see: M.S. Anderson, *Europe in the Eighteen Century 1713/1783* (London: Longman, 1961), chapter 8, 'Diplomacy and international relations'.

12 On this controversial concept of an international society see: Bull, *The Anarchical Society*; and, B.A. Roberson, *International Society and the Development of International Relations Theory* (London: Pinter, 1998).

13 See: James Mayall, *Nationalism and International Society* (Cambridge: Cambridge University Press, 1990).

14 Classically – L.F. Richardson in *Arms and Insecurity: A Mathematical Study of the Causes and Origins of War* (Pittsburgh, PA: Boxwood Press, 1960).

15 V.I. Lenin, *Imperialism, the Highest Stage of Capitalism* (1916, various editions).

16 Carl von Clausewitz, *On War* (translated and edited by M. Howard and P. Paret) (Princeton, NJ: Princetown University Press, 1976).

17 On which see: Inis L. Claude, *Swords into Ploughshares* (New York: Random House, 1964).

18 E.H. Carr, *The Twenty Years' Crisis, 1919–1939: An Introduction to the Study of International Relations* (London: Macmillan, 1939).

19 On which see also: H. Bull and A. Watson (eds), *The Expansion of International Society* (Oxford: Clarendon Press, 1984).

20 Karl W. Deutsch and J. David Singer, 'Multipolar power systems and international stability', *World Politics*, 16 (April 1964): 390–406.

21 Richard Rosecrance, 'Bipolarity, multipolarity, and the future', *Journal of Conflict Resolution*, 10 (September 1966): 314–27.

22 For varied discussions of the 'long peace' see: Charles W. Kegley, Jr (ed.), *The Long Postwar Peace: Contending Explanation and Projections* (New York: Harper Collins, 1991).

23 E.B. Haas, 'The balance of power: prescription, concept, or propaganda', *World Politics*, 5 (1953): 442–77.

24 For a summary of balance of power concepts see: Bull, *The Anarchical Society*, chapter 5.

25 Bull, *The Anarchical Society*.

26 Kaplan, *System and Process*; and Rosecrance, *Action and Reaction*.

27 Bull, *The Anarchical Society*.

28 Richardson, *Arms and Insecurity*.

29 See, especially, R.C. Snyder, H.W. Bruck and B. Sapin, *Foreign Policy Decision-Making: An Approach to the Study of International Politics* (New York: Free Press, 1962).

30 See, in particular: Kaplan, *System and Process in International Politics*; and Richard Rosecrance, *Action and Reaction in World Politics* (Boston: Little, Brown, 1963).

31 See: Morton Kaplan, 'The new great debate: traditionalism vs. science in international relations', *World Politics*, 19 (October 1966): 1–21.

32 Kaplan, *System and Process in International Politics*.
33 Essentially a cosmopolitan order, in which the general good is the primary value.
34 With one state effectively dominating the system.
35 A system lacking cosmopolitan values, any effective system-wide power, but with each state (or at least a number of significant states) able to deter any other from unpleasant behaviour.
36 For further details see: Kaplan, *System and Process*; or James E. Dougherty and Robert L. Pfaltzgraff, *Contending Theories of International Relations: A Comprehensive Survey* (New York: Harper & Row, 2nd edn, 1984, chapter 4. (Other chapters in other editions of this invaluable text.)
37 Particularly, Hedley Bull, 'The case for a classical approach', in K. Knorr and J.N. Rosenau (eds), *Contending Approaches to International Politics* (Princeton, NJ: Princeton University Press, 1969), pp. 20–38 (originally published in *World Politics*, April 1966).
38 Rosecrance, *Action and Reaction in World Politics*.
39 See: Chris Brown, *Understanding International Relations* (London: Macmillan, 1997), p. 105.
40 See, for an excellent overview: George Modelski and William R. Thomson, *Leading Sectors and World Powers* (Columbia, SC: University of South Carolina Press, 1996).
41 Snyder, Bruck and Sapin, *Foreign Policy Decision-making*.
42 Buzan, Jones and Little, *The Logic of Anarchy*.
43 For example: K.J. Holsti, *Peace and War: Armed Conflicts and International Order 1648–1989* (Cambridge: Cambridge University Press, 1991).
44 For example: Charles F. Doran, *Systems in Crisis: New Imperatives of High Politics at Century's End* (Cambridge: Cambridge University Press, 1991).
45 On which see: Carr, *The Twenty Years' Crisis*.
46 See, for example, J.W. Burton, *World Society* (Cambridge: Cambridge University Press, 1972); and M. Banks (ed.), *Conflict in World Society: A New Perspective on International Relations* (Brighton: Harvester/Wheatsheaf Books, 1984).
47 On the conditions for an effective Collective Security system see Claude, *Swords into Ploughshares*.
48 Brown, *Understanding International Relations*, p. 105.
49 See, for a critical discussion: R.J. Barry Jones, *The World Turned Upside Down?: Globalization and the Future of the State* (Manchester: Manchester University Press, 2000).

Further reading

Bull, H., *The Anarchical Society* (London: Macmillan, 1977). This is the classic statement of the 'international society' approach to international relations, in which the apparent anarchy of the international system is held to be moderated by the mutual accommodation of states in line with well-developed rules and norms of conduct and, in particular, the structure of international law.

Claude, I.L., *Power and International Relations* (New York: Random House, 1964). A seminal study of the idea of collective security – its necessary conditions and problematical prospects.

Haas, E.B., 'The balance of power: prescription, concept, or propaganda', *World Politics*, 5 (1953): 442–77. One of the basic reviews of the concept of the balance of power and its varied and ambigous meanings and usages.

Kaplan, M.A., *System and Process in International Politics* (New York: J. Wiley, 1957). A classical attempt to analyse balance of power systems in a 'scientific' manner.

Waltz, K.N., *Theory of International Politics* (London: Addison-Wesley, 1979). The statement of Neo-Realism by its founder.

5 Globalisation

Introduction

The idea of globalisation offers a sharp contrast to the 'traditional' realist, and other state focused views of international relations or the notion that the structure of the international political system is the overwhelmingly dominant factor in world affairs. At its most extreme – the 'strong globalisation thesis' – globalisation envisages a world system that has been transformed by the combined effects of a number of dominant forces and processes.[1] Modern technologies of transport, communication and information management have, in this view, facilitated an unprecedented level of world-wide financial, economic and even social integration. The effect has been to undermine the role of the 'traditional' nation state. Nation states, and their governments, are thus seen to be all but finished as effective economic actors, with little capacity to influence basic economic and industrial developments and with severely reduce abilities to run independent economic policies at the 'national' level.

A central problem with the globalisation view has to be acknowledged from the outset. This is the question of whether the term globalisation really applies to something that has already come into existence or whether it refers to a number of forces and processes that may be leading to a new global condition in the future. This question will be addressed later in the discussion of the globalisation approach and in critical references within discussions of the other major approaches to international relations.

Globalisation: patterns and processes

The evidence upon which it is possible to build a description of contemporary globalisation embraces both established conditions and the processes that underlie those conditions. The level of current financial integration thus involves relatively simple statements about such phenomena as the daily volume of financial flows and descriptions of the mechanisms through which such flows are directed. Financial integration is thus as much a matter of the physical connections amongst the firms and financial institutions in the world's leading financial centres as it is the transactions that they actually undertake on a daily basis. Such a duality is also characteristic of most of the other conditions and processes that are conventionally emphasised in discussions of globalisation, including the role and functioning of transnational corporations (TNCs), the general increase in levels of 'international' trade and the supposed emergence of a global culture or a global society.

Global financial integration

Some of the best evidence for the strong globalisation thesis is provided by the current level of global financial integration and the institutional arrangements which underlie that integration.[2] The exponential growth in the capacity and application of computer technology has permitted a massive increase in the speed with which financial transactions can be processed and the distances over which they can be conducted. Electronic trading systems are now commonplace in the stock exchanges of the world's leading financial centres, and, increasingly, in the new trading patterns amongst previously separate 'national' markets for stocks and shares. The speed of international trading in currencies and commodities has also been accelerated by the application of the same technologies. Communications via the internet are also enhancing the capacities of those engaged in a range of other financial services, including insurance.

The scale and speed of financial integration via the new technologies of computers and communications has been spurred by the wave of deregulation of financial services pursued by the governments of many of the world's leading economies during the 1980s and early 1990s and, more recently and with greater reservations, by the governments of a number of the newly industrialising countries (NICs). Such deregulation has permitted the emergence of a number of powerful financial enterprises. Boosted by new alliances and mergers within their home countries, these new financial monoliths have, via overseas acquisitions and/or the establishment of new foreign subsidiaries, been able to transcend the traditional separation of the world's leading financial centres.

The consequence of the new policy framework, the new technologies and the new ambitions of financial enterprises has been the massive expansion in the volume of international financial transaction. Financial flows across 'national' frontiers have, in particular, expanded massively during the past two to three decades. The precise volume of such transactions is changing so rapidly that an exact figure cannot be specified with any confidence. However, the ratio of annual transactions on foreign exchange markets to the value of world imports rose from approximately 2 to 1 in the mid 1960s to a ratio of some 85 to 1 by 1992.

The expansion in cross-border trade in stocks and shares (equities) has been equally impressive. The combined value of purchases of foreign equities by US investors and of US stocks and shares by foreign investors has grown from some $93 billion in 1980 to $1,523 billion by 1994: a growth rate of just over 16 times in 14 years.[3] The massive expansion in the scale of financial flows represented by the growth of foreign exchange dealings, and cross-border equity purchases, is clearly impressive and underlies many of the more extravagant claims about the level and significance of contemporary globalisation.

Transnational corporations, foreign direct investment and transitional production

Advocates of the globalisation perspective also emphasise the role of TNCs. Such corporations are defined by their ownership and control of subsidiaries in more than one country. In the late nineteenth century, TNCs were predominantly involved in producing and trading primary commodities like nitrates, copper, rubber or cocoa. By the late twentieth century, these traditional areas of TNC activity had been supplemented and overtaken by manufacturing goods for the consumers, industries and armies of the world and, increasingly, by the supply of sophisticated services.

TNCs have wide-ranging significance for the character and development of the global political economy. First, they are responsible for a growing share of international trade. Moreover, an increasing portion of international trade, probably somewhere between 40 and 50 per cent, now takes place *within* TNCs: intra-firm trade that, while crossing state frontiers, remains within the same company. This intra-firm trade is significant for a number of reasons: it reflects the extent of the transnational operations of such companies, and, significantly, it allows TNCs to exploit the mechanisms of transfer pricing to gain considerable tactical power in their dealings with 'national' governments, local businesses and labour organisations.

Transfer pricing is a function of the transnational mode of production or service supply that is increasingly characteristic of TNCs.[4] A company with subsidiaries in more than one country 'trades' with itself within its own organisation. It thus sets the 'prices' that each subsidiary charges other subsidiaries for its output to maximise the advantage to the parent company. TNCs, and their transnational mode of production and supply, are also central to much of the international diffusion of the most advanced production technologies; the international relocation of production, sometimes to areas of the world with lower labour costs; the steady growth of international economic transactions; the progressive erosion of the policy autonomy of governments; and the remorseless promotion of homogenous consumer tastes globally. The impact of TNCs in these respects rests upon the proportion of the world's production and sales of goods and services for which they are responsible. By the late 1980s TNCs accounted for some 25–30 per cent of the GDP of the market economies and sales by their overseas affiliates had risen to $4 trillion, equalling the value of conventional exports of goods and services world-wide.[5] Such a powerful position in production and supply is reflected, and sustained by, the TNCs' domination of much of the world's research and development in the most advanced sectors of industrial innovation, production and extraction. When further reinforced by the increasing levels of international operation, and international sourcing of components, by major producers in many industries, particularly, motor vehicles, chemicals, construction and electronics, the structural impact of TNCs in the contemporary world economy is difficult to exaggerate.

The influence of TNCs is not confined to their role in international production, trade and supply. The clear interests that TNCs have in the elimination of restrictions upon economic activity is such as to make them powerful advocates of a reduced economic role for governments, the further deregulation of economic activity and the progress towards ever-greater liberalisation of international trade and financial transactions. TNCs have thus been major advocates of greater globalisation as much as they have been mere reflections of globalizing forces that are beyond their interests and influence.

Information technology and modern telecommunications

World-wide telecommunications' networks that connect and integrate a myriad of formerly unconnected centres of decision making and information processing are a central feature of contemporary globalisation. These networks are central both to international financial integration and to the enhanced capabilities and opportunities of TNCs. They are also, themselves, a definitive feature of contemporary globalisation.[6]

The increasing use, and the enhanced capability, of modern telecommunications systems, and the components from which they are created, has accelerated at a phenomenal rate since the mid-1970s, when the modern micro-electronics revolution exploded out of the military sector and swept into commercial and personal life. The power of the microprocessors and memory modules that are incorporated into today's personal computers, and in many dedicated consumer and commercial applications, has expanded at such a rate that everyday devices now far exceed the capabilities of the mainframe computers that directed the first US manned moon-shot.

When allied to an increasing density of communications networks, such computing and information processing capabilities mark an unprecedented advance in the capacity of human beings to communicate with one another, to base decisions upon massive quantities of disparate information and to control developments in the most remote parts of the world. Internationally integrated financial trading rests upon, and exemplifies, just such massive advances in communications and information processing capabilities as do the internal communications and control systems of many TNCs.

Globalisation and the coming of world cities

The progressive integration of the world's financial system and productive structures, through computer-based communications and information processing systems, may be altering the role and status of a number of the world's leading cities. Formerly functioning to serve the needs of their home societies, by providing central government, core financial services and the headquarters of many of the leading enterprizes, the more prominent of such leading cities may now be increasingly orientated towards servicing the global economy. World cities[7] may thus resist the trend towards urban flight and retain a central role in the new world system. A plethora of specialised services and international business, in such areas as economic analysis, advertising, transport services and financial advice will continue to flourish in the leading cities and to support the activities of the headquarters of major TNCs and financial enterprizes.

The 'world city' will continue to survive as a real, physical entity because of the benefits of personal interaction amongst those who play central roles in the varied enterprizes that are at the core of its economic activities. In these cities, it will be possible to meet, share knowledge and to establish valuable contacts. However, the key players in the core industries of the 'world cities' will be increasingly at home in a transnational network of fellow professionals as they will be within their home city and society. Modern transport and communications combine to facilitate continuing contact over a geographical range that was previously impossible.

Contemporary transport systems

Advances in information processing and international communications' capabilities have been so phenomenal within the last three decades of the twentieth century that observers have sometimes been tempted to believe that every human need can be satisfied through the personal computer, the internet or a mobile phone. The realities of much of life, however, rest upon the satisfaction of human needs for real goods and those services that can be provided only through direct, physical contact. Advances in the scale and sophistication of the transport industry thus remains central to contemporary globalisation.

Progress in transport has been most visible to most people in the rapid improvement and expansion of air transport. The air transport 'revolution' lies at the heart of the massive post-war expansion of popular tourism and of business travel. Increasing numbers of manufactured goods are also shipped by air freight, particularly those with high value and relatively low weight or bulk.

The world's maritime industry has also witnessed steady advances in recent decades. Bulk products, like fuels and grains, are now shipped around the world in ships that are, by historical standards, massive. Containers are becoming a norm for international maritime transport and, with their arrival, cargo handling has become increasingly computer controlled. Traditional docks have been steadily replaced by larger, more mechanised, deep-water container terminals that, for all their distance from established centres of population, continue to be of profound importance for the societies that they serve. Thus, shipping employs proportionally fewer seamen and dock workers than in earlier decades but is responsible for a steadily rising volume of commodities, components and finished goods.

Global social integration and a new global culture

With the advent of the new global networks of information, the rise of global broadcasting enterprises, the extended opportunities for personal travel and the steady increase in international shipments of goods and provision of services, many believe that a new stage has been reached in global social integration and the emergence of a new global culture. Evidence for the new global society[8] is to be found in the vast increase in interpersonal contacts in today's world, by telephone, internet or physical meetings. The people who interact within this new global social arena increasingly wear the same styles of clothes, drive the same models of cars, consume the new multinational cuisine and watch the same films and television programmes. The language of this new global society is increasingly English. The borderless interpersonal contact and communication of the new global society is thus intimately associated with the other manifestations of a globalised world: at once, both symptoms of such globalisation and an important contribution to its further progress. The addition of this new global society to the effects of the other dimensions of contemporary globalisation underlies, in the view of many observers, the weakening of the role and capacity of the nation state and its imminent demise as a central focus for economic and even political life.[9]

Globalisation: symptoms (causes?)

- Increased levels of international trade
- Increased levels of international financial flows
- Increased levels of foreign direct investment
- Increased levels of international travel
- Increased levels of international communication
- Increased international spread of cultural 'products'
- Emergence of a new transnational elite

Sources

The origins of contemporary globalisation are both complex and controversial. The central debate is between those who believe that the progress of globalisation is irresistible and driven by impersonal forces and those who argue, in contrast, that the developments that constitute contemporary globalisation are both reversible and the product of clear human influences.

Globalisation as an inevitable process

Arguments that increasing globalisation is inevitable and irresistible highlight a variety of causes. Two of the most commonly identified causes are the inherent dynamics of capitalist economics and the effects of technological progress. The view that the inherent dynamic of capitalist economics generates increasing globalisation is common to many liberal economists and to some kinds of neo-Marxists.

'LIBERAL' PERSPECTIVES ON GLOBALISATION

Free-market-orientated 'liberal' theorists of the inevitable advance of globalisation stress the dynamic nature and effects of the free-enterprise and the free-trade system. With the steady reduction of barriers to enterprise and to trade, societies are increasingly able to produce a wide range of goods and services for which they can find buyers in the world market. Societies are equally able to purchase goods and services from any source within an increasingly wide world market. Firms are also ever-more able to take advantage of international production opportunities, to exploit economies of scale through increasingly internationalised patterns of production and to serve an increasingly integrated world market. Competitive pressures, indeed, ensure that firms that do respond positively to such new opportunities will be the companies that prosper and survive and that may grow into leading TNCs. The result of such opportunities is thus the rapid development of a genuinely world-wide market, supplied by firms that are increasingly orientated towards a global market and organised on an international basis: a globalised free-market economy that brings profit to firms, employment opportunities to the world's work force and enhanced consumer satisfaction to the world's population.[10]

RADICAL CRITICS OF GLOBALISATION

Radical critics of globalisation, including a number of neo-Marxists, acknowledge many of the same sources of advancing globalisation as do liberal globalists, but emphasise means and motives that are viewed in a less benign light. The radical view rests upon the general proposition that the competitive pressures of the free-market system confront capitalist enterprises with the interlinked imperatives of cost cutting, expansion of production and ceaseless market seeking. Such firms inhabit a 'Darwinian' world in which the big swallow the small and the quick outrun the slow in an ever-intensifying competitive struggle for survival.[11]

The problems of capital accumulation in a highly competitive context is thus central to the behaviour of all capitalist enterprises. Complacency and stagnation spell decline and ultimate dissolution in the competitive economy, and can be avoided only through the ceaseless confrontation, and defeat, of competitors, through the tireless pursuit of cheaper production, productive investment, new products and new markets. Transnational corporations arise as the inevitable consequence of such competitive pressures. However, the measures adopted in the ceaseless competitive struggle mean constant downward pressures on profits and ultimate viability. The 'laws' of capitalist competition and capital accumulation thus drive a linked process of ceaseless expansion and faltering profitability. The firms caught up in such an economic maelstrom are thus drawn remorselessly towards ultimate self-destruction and, with them, the destruction of the socio-economic system that they represent.

The inherent dynamic and ultimate contradiction of the capitalist process may be modified, in practice, by the formation of 'hegemonic blocs' – implicit alliances of politicians, business leaders and opinion formers – which serve the apparent requirements of the capitalist system and the immediate interests of its dominant classes. Followers of the Italian Marxist, Antonio Gramsci, see such a hegemonic bloc as embracing the formal political and economic institutions of the capitalist state; the prevalent ideology, which is shared by capitalist and most non-capitalists alike; and the civil society which exists in a formally separate, but functionally complementary, manner to the capitalist state. The ideology and institutions of hegemonical capitalism are, under suitable conditions, capable of expanding their area of influence throughout the international system and generating a global capitalist hegemony.[12] The current phase of advancing globalisation could be seen, from such a Neo-Gramscian perspective, as just such a period of intensifying global capitalist hegemony.[13]

Remorseless globalisation can thus be as much the product of a world cast in the mould of radical critiques of international market capitalism and of one reflecting the vision of the liberal globalists.

'REALIST' VIEWS OF GLOBALISATION

The role of TNCs in contemporary globalisation can also be viewed from a broadly 'Realist' perspective. Firms, like all other actors in a competitive or conflictful environment, are seen to be directed by the twin objectives of profit and power. These are central to the ultimate success of competitive enterprises and drive their advance to global scales of operation. Profit provides the resources for investment, diversification, expansion and internationalisation. Power comes with the acquisition and retention of dominant positions in the market, as buyer or seller, and such positions, once achieved, can lead to the accumulation of abundant profits, as the spectacular record of the Microsoft software corporations has demonstrated.[14]

The protection of initial competitive advantages that have been secured for new products or processes may be essential to secure sufficient returns to cover development costs by innovative firms. The 'product cycle'[15] of industrial innovations, from *introductory*, to *mature*, to *standardised* phase may impel the innovative firm into a form of aggressive defence once maturation, and then standardisation, begin to take place: to take over emergent competitors at home and abroad and thereby preserve the dominant market position enjoyed during the introductory phase. Such forms of counter-competitive behaviour may give way to more aggressive forms of offensive where a sufficient level of product differentiation can be established, as in the case of computer software, and can sustain the pre-emptive exclusion of potential competitors.[16]

Realists do not, however, accept either the autonomy or the primacy of economic processes. The economic developments that are associated with globalisation, including the activities of TNCs, are thus seen to be closely inter-related with political processes and purposes. Minimally, an international system that is fragmented into formally sovereign states still constitutes the basic context within which world-wide economic processes and development take place. Effective world-wide political control and legal jurisdiction is compromised by this fragmentation of legitimate authority and regulative capacity.[17]

States have also acted in such a way as to promote the growing internationalisation of economic activity. The leading states during the decades immediately following the Second World War actively promoted an increasingly liberal, free-trade system internationally. The International Monetary Fund (IMF) and the International Bank for Reconstruction and Development (the World Bank) were established at the Bretton Woods Conference in 1944 to provide the post-war international economy with a stable financial system. The General Agreement on Tariffs and Trade (GATT) of 1947 was then concluded and deployed, in the absence of a more effective mechanism, to promote the progressive liberalisation of international trade.[18] Such general measures were further reinforced by the substantial support that the United States of America provided for post-war economic recovery amongst the industrialised nations through the Marshall Aid Programme.

The conscious promotion of economic recovery and liberalisation during the post-war decades provided the basis for gradual, although far from complete, progress towards a world-wide free-trade system. A range of further motives, decisions and non-decisions, however, fertilised the roots of prospective globalisation. Many of the leading industrial states identified their interests with those of their leading companies and thus provided considerable support for the overseas activities and investments of those companies. Such support was sometimes prompted by concerns about access to the raw materials and energy sources that such companies extracted and shipped back to their 'home' counties. However, support for the foreign activities of companies often reflected a general 'neo-mercantilist' notion[19] of the desirability of securing profits and foreign exchange from such activities. In some cases support for overseas investment also reflected a sense that general economic strength and industrial competitiveness could be preserved, and enhanced, by the work of such transnationally active companies.

Financial integration remains one of the most advanced forms of globalisation. The conditions for such integration have, however, also been encouraged, intentionally and unintentionally, by states and their governments.[20] Liquidity in the international financial system was substantially boosted by the huge and persistent balance of payments deficits that the United States of America ran, particularly during the era of the Vietnam War. Domestic financial controls within the United States of America also encourage many of its leading banks, and other financial institutions, to engage in offshore financial activity, particularly within Europe, and created, in so doing, the Euro-dollar market. This development was further encouraged by the wish of the government of the Soviet Union to retain its holdings of the US dollar outside the United States during a period of political sensitivity and concerns about the security of such holdings if retained within the USA.

The fashion for economic liberalisation, that became dominant from the early 1980s onwards, also encouraged policies of financial deregulation within many of the world's leading economies. Such deregulation embraced the abolition of exchange controls by many leading economies; the removal of restrictions on participation in domestic financial systems by foreign firms; permission for new international mergers of, and alliances amongst, financial enterprises; the wide-spread introduction of information technologies and their associated networks; and, finally, the emergence of twenty-four, internationally integrated, markets for currencies, equities and a range of other financial instruments.

Many of the most prominent features of contemporary globalisation did not, therefore, emerge purely spontaneously. States and governments played an important, and often critical, role in establishing many of the conditions that permitted increasing international trade and financial integration and, in some cases, provided them with positive encouragement. Many of these actions, and their effects, were intentional; others, however, were unintentional and their consequences little understood.

TECHNOLOGY AND GLOBALISATION

The contrasting perspectives upon contemporary globalisation reflect different views of the relationship between economic factors and forces and those residing within the political domain. Technology also occupies a complex and controversial position within contemporary globalisation and its analysis.

Elements of technological determinism are common to some advocates of both liberal and radical views of globalisation. This notion of technological determinism involves the idea, often implicit rather than explicit, that globalisation is being driven forward, inexorably, by the development and deployment of a number of the new technologies that have risen to prominence in recent years. The new means for gathering, processing and transmitting information are

Competing views of globalisation

Liberal

- Globalisation marks the further development of the free-market international division of labour, bringing greater efficiency, choice and prosperity
- Globalisation will bring the progressive equalisation of wealth and well-being worldwide
- Globalisation has reduced, and will continue to reduce, the role of the state in the provision of economic well-being

Radical

- Globalisation marks the global extension and intensification of capitalist exploitation
- Globalisation postpones, but cannot delay indefinitely, the ultimate collapse of unstable capitalism
- Globalisation has been assisted by sympathetic governments, but will further undermine their capacity for regulation and economic provision

Realist

- Globalisation is an uneven phenomenon, that has enhanced the power and influence of some groups and societies at the expense of others
- Globalisation has been created, substantially, by the leading states and their firms
- Globalisation creates a complex situation from the point of view of governments and their regulative activities: compromising some, but enhancing the need and capacity for action in others

attributed particular importance in this respect, although the increasing speed and decreasing costs of international transport are also deemed to be significant.

Technological innovations, particularly information technology, have clearly been significant to contemporary globalisation. The problem, however, is to differentiate real causes from those conditions that merely assist, or provide opportunities, for developments that have other, and possibly deeper, causes. Many contemporary technologies clearly facilitate financial integration, a growing scale and density of international trade and increased mobility of peoples, but they many not, in themselves, *cause* such developments. Indeed, the pressures for many of the technological innovations, particularly in the speed and nature of their deployment, may be a product of factors and forces within the wider political and economic systems.

GLOBAL PROBLEMS AND GLOBAL RESPONSES

The emergence of a range of problems that are common to the whole of humanity has also been identified as a growing source of globalisation in social interaction and governance. The effects of the growth-orientated world economy lie at the heart of many of these perceived problems. Growing pollution, resource exhaustion, over-crowding and general damage to the global ecology are often attributed to the current patterns of industrial production and material consumption.

Such intensifying environmental problems are believed, by advocates of both global governance and social globalisation, to generate a new awareness of the needs for global-level responses to problems that have assumed a global scale and to stimulate intensifying cross-border contacts amongst the growing numbers of those who have become concerned about the looming threats to human and environmental survival.[21] Environmental concerns have clearly grown in recent years and have fused with the possibilities presented by the technologies of contact and communication to stimulate the growth of transnational networks of environmentally concerned groups and individuals. The Rio Conference on the environment, and its projected successors, also attest to some increase in sensitivity to environmental issues at the level of state governments.

Transborder contacts have also been encouraged amongst those who are concerned about other aspects of contemporary economic developments, including the possible marginalisation of many groups of workers in both industrialised and less developed countries (LDCs).

GLOBAL SOCIETY AND GLOBAL CULTURE

Many also believe that the possibilities presented by modern technologies, with the intensification of international trade and the spread of transnational enterprize are fusing to generate a global society with a new global culture. Modern communication technologies are believed to be generating a new mutual awareness amongst the world's populations. Such communications are also confronting people in all corners of the globe with common images, promoting common consumer goods and stimulating common responses to a range of issues. The intensification of international trade and competitions is, in its turn, bringing the same consumer goods to a wider proportion of the world's population, while economic growth is providing more and more people with the income with which to purchase the goods and services that are now available.

A new global consumer culture is the first, and most obvious, consequence of such developments. Globalists, however, also believe that the increasingly common experiences of economic life, consumption patterns and technologically facilitated contacts and communications are also stimulating growing homogenisation within human culture in general. Formerly distinct societies will, in this view, increasingly come to adopt common beliefs, values and expectations.[22] The benign consequences of such cultural homogenisation will be the growth of common sympathy and understanding, with a consequential reduction, and eventual disappearance, of culturally based misunderstandings, suspicions and hostilities.

The question confronting expectations of enhanced global governance, or extended social and cultural globalisation, is whether needs and possibilities necessarily generate the outcomes anticipated. The automatic linkage of needs with results, in a positive manner, is at the heart of the functionalist approach to human affairs and to change in human behaviour and institutions in particular. Such functionalism is, however, a highly controversial and deeply contested perspective upon the human condition, which also accords poorly with the turbulent and destructive history of humanity.

The issue here is whether invention and innovation in the technical sphere is driven purely by its own logic, or whether invention and innovation is more frequently encouraged by powerful forces within the wider social, economic and political system. Much of the pace and direction of technical innovation in early modern Europe certainly reflected the pressures created by a process of ceaseless political and military competition and conflict amongst its emergent states. Innovations in military technology were encouraged by the need to secure military advantage over adversaries; systems of large-scale manufacture reflected the problems of equipping increasingly large armies and navies; and developments in systems of government and financial management were prompted by the need to supply and finance armed forces. The state-sponsored invention of the accurate clock, or chronometer, as a basis for accurate maritime navigation has been well documented in Dava Sobel's *Longitude*.[23]

The example of early modern Europe thus illustrates the complex relationship between context and innovation. Innovations offer those who might apply them with new, and often powerful, possibilities. However, such innovations need to be appropriate to the needs of the those who might apply them, must be recognised as appropriate and then applied successfully. Moreover, economies, political and military systems may actually signal their needs and desires to innovators and stimulate, thereby, inventions that meet those needs. However, many technological innovations, once introduced, may find applications and have effects, far beyond the intentions or expectations of those who sought their initial introduction. The government of the USA provided a major stimulus to the development of micro-electronics from the early 1960s onwards, through massive provisions of research and development finance focused precisely on areas of innovation within electronics and information processing;[24] the unintended and unexpected consequence was the explosion of computing capability, the spread of the personal computer, the internet and the coming of world-wide information networks.

The technological imperative is thus a complex issue. Many innovations are positively encouraged by aspects of the context within which they occur. Innovations need to be taken up and applied, and may be neglected by intention or oversight. Innovations, once introduced, do, however, create possibilities that may be difficult to forego by those who wish to preserve or enhance their profits, power or position. It is the complex interconnection between dynamic economic and political systems, on the one hand, and a system of ceaseless technological innovation, on the other, that gives technologically based globalisation is apparently automatic and irreversible character.

Problems and solutions

The benign view of globalisation identifies a wide range of benefits with the further progress of globalisation, in its economic, political and social manifestations. Economic globalisation will, it is believed, reflect and encourage the full integration of the world's economy. Competition will hold sway world-wide. Consumers will be provided with the widest range of goods and services and the lowest possible prices. Producers will have the strongest incentives to specialise in the production and supply of those goods or services for which they are best suited. All obstacles to economic innovation and efficiency will be swept away. For optimists, the cumulative effect of these processes and conditions will be a world in which sustained growth and ever-improving human well-being will be combined with the final defeat of the scourge of inflation and consequential economic dislocation: the 'new economy' of some observers of the contemporary United States of America. The operation of the free-market system will provide automatic solutions to any problems that might arise.

Politically, advancing globalisation will both require and facilitate the emergence of more effective forms of governance at the global level. Managing and regulating a financially and economically integrated world effectively will require the reinforcement of established forms of international governance or the invention of new, and possibly supranational, institutions. Such pressures will be reinforced by the growing problems of global environmental management and preservation. The rivalries of states will thus be challenged and overwhelmed by the needs of a more globally integrated world. Recent progress towards political integration on a regional basis will thus be replicated at the global level.

Socially, new possibilities for contact across traditional state frontiers, and the growing range of issues attracting cross-border contacts, will stimulate growing and intensifying social networks on a global scale. Such an emergent global society will, in turn, contribute to the development of a new global culture, in which core values and expectations will develop and common life patterns and tastes will gradually crystallise.

This benign view is not, however, shared by all those who reflect upon contemporary globalisation and its future impact. A range of observers, from neo-Marxists, of various types, to sceptical economic Realists, believe, in sharp contrast, that many of the processes and developments that have been identified with globalisation confront the populations of many societies with substantial problems and carry, as a consequence, serious dangers of economic, environmental, social and, ultimately, political danger.

Instability in a financially integrated world

PROBLEMS

Globalisation is often held to be most advanced in the international financial system. World-bestriding financial firms and twenty-four hour trading within and amongst the world's leading stock exchanges and financial centres have combined to create a picture of an increasingly seamless world financial system. The sheer scale of financial flows across international boundaries is now so great as to place governments under severe pressures and constraints and, in the extreme, to threaten the economic and financial system of the whole world with serious instability.[25]

Rapid flows of money into and out of national currencies can now undermine the value of those currencies, and destroy their participation in international currency stabilisation arrangements within short periods of time, as the enforced withdrawal of the UK from the Exchange Rate Mechanism (ERM) of the European Community on 16 September 1992 demonstrated.

Transactions in international currency markets, on the stock exchanges of the major trading nations and on a range of markets for commodities and financial instruments (like derivatives)[26] is now also on a scale, and at a speed, such that the well-being, and even survival, of major financial institutions can be undermined within relatively short periods of time when mistakes, or dubious practices, are initiated by their employees, as demonstrated by both the collapse of Barings Bank and the Sumitomo Bank's massive losses from rogue trading on the world Copper market.

Major financial disasters of this type, have reinforced the earlier concerns about the ultimate stability of the world's financial system that were prompted by the emergence of the less developed countries' debt crisis in 1982. By the early 1980s a number of LDCs, particularly within Latin America, had accumulated massive loans from a wide range of the leading financial institutions of the advanced industrial countries (AICs) to. A combination of factors, including collapsing markets for the LDCs' primary exports and rapid increases in international interest rates, confronted many of the borrowers with levels of repayment that could not now be met. The prospect of debt default thus arose, and faced the financial institutions of the AICs with potential losses on a scale that threatened their collapse. The alarm and activity generated within the AICs in the early half of the 1980s demonstrated the seriousness of the situation. It also illustrated the complex patterns of interconnection and mutual dependence that had grown up and that now characterised the financial relations of the contemporary international system.

The dangers generated by the contemporary level of world financial integration thus turn upon the possibilities that problems starting in one location, or in one financial relationship, with damage to one financial institutions be transmitted throughout the rest of the system; with the possible collapse of one financial institution precipitation the progressive collapse of other institutions with which it is connected.[27]

SOLUTIONS

The speed and scale of financial flows, that have accompanied the emergence of a highly integrated global financial system, has thus created problems for individual societies , and their governments, and for the global system as a whole. Governance of this complex and highly interconnected financial system has traditionally been undertaken by mixture of private and public authorities operating at both 'national' and international levels. In the private domain, governance has been undertaken by such 'national' institutions as stock exchanges and by a range of associations and committees that have been created to review matters of common concern and to formulate common principles and standards. In the public domain, governance at the national level has been the province of state governments and such linked agencies as central banks and agencies for the regulation of banking and investment industries. At the international level, there are a range of organisations from the various 'Groups' of major states, the International Monetary Fund and the World Bank and long-standing agencies like the Bank for International Settlements.[28]

Private regulation has a potential role in the governance of the new global financial system. The influence of nationally based private governance in the financial system will be largely confined to the economy within which the relevant authorities are operating, with the partial exception of those operating within the world's leading 'national' economies.

The creation of new, global standards for accountancy has been the subject of considerable work by representatives of 'national' stock exchanges and other interested financial institutions. Such standards would be clearly helpful for international investors as they would ensure comparable criteria for the profitability, or otherwise, of businesses located in different countries. Such private governance is, however, focused primarily upon matters of specific interest to the businesses represented in such institutions of private international governance and tends to produce significant measures of self-restraint (and hence short-term costs) only when something has already gone seriously wrong and when such measures are the only way to restore levels of public confidence in the financial sector that has already been badly damaged by scandal or disaster.

The problem created by the new level of global financial integration in the domain of public governance is that it has overwhelmed the capacity of the great majority of purely national level authorities – public or private – to provide effective oversight and regulation of the financial transactions that are important for both their own economies and societies or for the wider international system. Only the governments and private authorities of the economically most powerful states – like the USA – or amalgams of states – like the European Union – retain any real capacity for unilateral action and effect upon the wider international financial system. Effective unilateral action by such major economic actors would, however, be costly in the short term. The freedom of action of locally based financial institutions might have to be restrained, short-term profits might be reduced, firms and investors might be prompted to relocate abroad, and the government might find its access to credit diminished. The effectiveness of unilateral attempts to impose new regulations upon the international financial system and, if necessary, to restructure it in more manageable directions, would ultimately rest upon the need of private financial institutions to do business with the economy of the assertive government. The bargaining relationship between private financial institutions and an assertive government would, in turn, be increased substantially in the government's favour if the governments of other major economies adopted similar policies and measures.

Effective public governance of the financial system at the international level revolves, in large part, around cooperation amongst 'national' governments and, hence, within various international organisations. Such co-operation, however, may be constrained by one, or both, of two obstacles. The first is relatively straightforward, but none the less serious. It is the inability of some governments to accept the necessity of substantive regulation of the international financial system. Ideological influences may be such as to convince some governments, at least in the short term, that an unconstrained international financial system will spontaneously generate generally beneficial outcomes and avoid serious instability. Governments under the influence of such ultra-liberal beliefs will clearly reject cooperative efforts at international regulation and control of the financial sector.

Difficulties can be encountered, however, even when most (if not all) governments are agreed upon the principle of some regulation of international financial transactions. It is all too tempting for governments to conclude that such regulation would be desirable but that it would be best if other societies took the lead in developing and applying the appropriate rules and, thereby, incur the primary costs. If successful, such a 'free-riding' state obtains the benefits of effective international financial regulation while minimising the costs that it has to bear directly. If the regulatory initiative is unsuccessful, such 'free riders' save themselves the costs that have been invested in the failed experiment. Free riding of this type is all too common a temptation in international relations, where many of the conventional constraints[29] upon such a practice are largely absent.

An extreme case occurs within the contemporary international financial system where some states are able to secure disproportionate advantages for themselves precisely because other states – unilaterally or collectively – are attempting to regulate (or tax) financial enterprizes that operate within their jurisdictions. Such 'offshore havens' provide low tax and 'no questions' locations within which financial (and other) enterprises can register their headquarters and nominally lodge their accounts and other financial reports. Such 'offshore havens' thus facilitate tax avoidance, the evasion of inspection and regulation and have, in the extreme, provided the ideal location for organising the large-scale 'laundering' of drug profits and other dubious financial transfers. The 'collective good' of ensuring honest and responsible international financial transactions is thus undermined by the free riding of offshore tax havens, while the incentives for the creation of such havens are actually enhanced by the very effort to ensure effective financial regulation by the more responsible states and their governments.

The existence of free-riding tax havens reinforces the need for vigorous unilateral action by the leading economies to establish rules for the international financial system and to enforce it, if necessary, by exerting compelling pressures upon recalcitrant states and companies, as began to happen during 2000. Such efforts would clearly be substantially enhanced by wide-spread cooperation on the creation and implementation of such regulation amongst the leading economies and within the major institutions of public international financial governance.

Competition and control in a world of transnational corporations

PROBLEMS

Business enterprises that operate across state frontiers in many economic and industrial sectors are also a fundamental part of contemporary globalisation and create their own particular pressures and problems. Attention has often been drawn to the sheer size of many such TNCs and the positions of power and influence that they occupy in many global industries.

Size, wealth and market power are certainly powerful assets in the armouries of many TNCs in their dealings with customers, suppliers, competitors and, indeed, governments. Size and market position often endow TNCs with monopoly power, enabling them to set prices, technical standards and the rate of technological innovation. The dominant market position of TNCs in many industries may, in turn, confront governments with difficult choices if they wish those industries to operate within their countries. In the extreme the TNCs may be able to dictate many of the basic terms under which they will set up, or maintain, operations within any state.

Wealth also gives many TNCs a general asset which can be deployed widely to influence popular attitudes, to purchase influence and, in the extreme, to finance subversion against, or the armed overthrow of, unsympathetic governments. TNCs generally limit themselves to the pursuit of influence within stable democracies and well-developed industrial economies. The fragile political systems and weaker economies of many LDCs have, however, often left them open to the more dubious forms of pressure from TNCs, with TNC funded subversion in many Latin American countries in the 1950s and 1960s and notorious TNC involvements in the civil wars in the Congo in 1960 and Nigeria during 1967–70.

The structural advantages of TNCs are, however, the decisive advantages in their relations with governments, and the source of greatest problems for sovereign states and the clearest evidence of their significance to globalisation. The transnational mode of activity of such TNCs encourages a footloose approach to the location of their economic activities and, unless there are decisive locational constraints such as the sources of rare raw materials, reinforces their capacity for flexible sourcing of inputs and, facilitates their transfer pricing.

Footloose TNCs have played a significant part in the relocation of economic activity, and the international diffusion of technology, that has been accelerating in recent decades. This process of relocation and technology diffusion is not without its benefits for the members of those societies to which production is relocated and technology transferred. 'Losing' societies may, however, be faced with a variety of difficulties by such processes. Jobs opportunities may be significantly affected if a large TNC relocates some of its manufacturing activities, with past studies indicating a significant loss of 'blue-collar' jobs, with some increase in 'white-collar' and managerial posts. Government tax revenues may begin to drop precipitously. The balance of trade and of payments may suffer significantly. The well-being of a network of former suppliers may be seriously damaged by the departure of such enterprises, with significant longer-term effects upon the industrial capacity of the economy.

Transnational operations also encourage firms to take advantage of a range of sourcing opportunities around the world. This allows goods and services to be provided more cheaply to consumers, but may replicate, and even reinforce, many of the effects associated with the relocation of the primary economic and industrial activity of the TNC, as jobs in a range of firms and industries are effectively 'exported' to new locations around the world.

Transfer pricing remains a decisive advantage for TNCs, and a serious challenge to effective governance, within a world in which governments and regulation continues to be divided amongst sovereign states. The ability to set the 'prices' for shipments of components and services within its geographically distributed system allows the TNC to evade a number of constraints created by state governments. Thus, if subsidiaries are located in countries that have different rates of taxation on profits made locally, a company may overprice the goods or services shipped to the subsidiary in the highest tax country and/or under price the goods or services that it, in turn, ships on to subsidiaries in other countries. Whichever pricing tactic is adopted, the net effect is to reduce, or even eliminate, the apparent profit made by the subsidiary in the high tax country and to make that profit reappear in the accounts of one or more of the company's subsidiaries in lower tax countries.

Tax avoidance is only one of the consequences of transfer pricing within TNCs. Transfer pricing is also a major mechanism for the avoidance of controls upon the movement of money into or out of a country, by making such movements appear to be no more than the necessary payments for, or receipts from, trade in goods or services. Money can also be shipped through the transfer pricing mechanism into a country in which the government is trying to restrain growth and investment as part of a counter-inflationary policy. Conversely, a company can surreptitiously remove its investments in any country and transfer them to the subsidiaries in a country in which it wishes to reinvest its resources. Transfer pricing is thus a prime example of, and a major mechanism through which, the operations of TNCs have reduced the effectiveness of governments in the area of 'national' economic, and industrial, policy and left them increasingly exposed to pressures from the wider global economy.

SOLUTIONS

The problems generated by TNCs in the extractive, manufacturing and service sectors are broadly similar to those created by the international financial system. TNCs are able to take advantage of off-shore havens for registration and use their transnational mode of organisation to negate 'national' rules and evade 'national' taxes. Centrally coordinated policies and actions across a number of states may also allow a TNC to adopt 'divide and rule' strategies against the governments of the states in which they operate or are considering operating. Such 'divide and rule' strategies can be used to secure ever-higher subsidies from governments and to extract concessions over a range of operational conditions, including employment laws and pollution regulations. The weakness of many TNCs, when compared to purely financial enterprises, is that their physical capital is necessarily located within the territories, and their markets are the populations of states.

The locational restraints upon TNCs reduce, but do not eliminate, their advantages in relationship to the wholly locationally constrained governments of existing states. Similar considerations and constraints thus affect the governance of TNCs' activities, private and public, 'national' and international as those that arise in the financial arena. TNCs may be affected by private self-regulation within specific industrial sectors within some states. International private governance may exist where firms seek to control the world market for specific products or resources through the establishment of a regulatory cartel. Such private governance at the 'national' and international level is, however, primarily self-regarding and usually reactive to, rather than anticipatory of, problems or dangers.

Effective public governance of TNCs is problematical at the 'national' level. Their transnational mode of operation allows TNCs to evade the control of the governments of most economies. Only where an economy provides a TNC with a particularly valuable resource or market, or is the location of important, and relatively immobile, physical capital, is the TNC vulnerable to pressures from a government or regulative authority, that recognises its bargaining advantages and is disposed to exploit them in its relations with the TNC.

International public governance of TNCs and their activities encounters exactly the same difficulties of ideological constraint, free riding and the disproportionate gains for permissive states that compromise efforts to establish effective international regulation of the international financial system.

The intensification of international competition

PROBLEMS

The developments and forces that have been driving globalisation are combining to intensify the scale and intensity of competition within the world economy. New technologies of communication and information processing are, themselves, allowing the more rapid and effective international diffusion of technology, know-how, information and knowledge about market conditions. All but the most specialised of products are now produced in a large number of economies, including the NICs of South East Asia and Latin America, and exported vigorously into the international market. The products that were formerly the exclusive province of the AICs – motor cars, sophisticated electrical and electronic equipment – are now produced and exported by a wider range of economies. Only in advanced military equipment, in larger civilian airliners, in the production of the more exotic chemicals and materials, and in the innovation of cutting-edge technologies and products do the established AICs retain any kind of monopoly of production and supply.

SOLUTIONS

Many societies, particularly the AICs, display ambivalent responses to the intensification of international competition. Policies have been adopted to enhance the economic and industrial competitiveness of those societies that have experienced increased foreign competition, with emphasis upon investment, industrial innovation, and education and training.[30] However, such societies have simultaneously been prey to protectionist and mercantilist impulses. Domestic industries have been protected with tariffs, quotas and a variety of associated measures to restrain imports. Exports have equally been supported with subsidies and officially sponsored promotional campaigns. Such protectionist and mercantilist measures, however, may have a contagious character and a zero (or even negative) sum effect; other states are likely to adopt counter-measures, thereby denying the protectionist or mercantilist state the advantages that it sought.

Accelerating rates of economic and industrial change

PROBLEMS

Closely linked to the intensification of international economic competition is the acceleration of the rate of change within economic and industrial life. This acceleration of change also reflects the influences of the technologies – primarily computers and information processing – that both ease international diffusion and reduce the costs of adopting new systems of production and of entering new areas of production and supply. Computers and information technology play a central role in accelerated communications, in new manufacturing systems and in the expanding range of products to which computers, in one guise or another, are now integral.

Changes in the attitudes of management, and in the expectations and capabilities of their work forces, have reflected the intensification of international competition and the acceleration of change. Management now expects to face rapid and forceful competition in any product area in which it might have achieved a temporary lead. Work forces increasingly expect to have to be adaptable and to adjust rapidly to new tasks and techniques. A culture of flexibility, in which education and training make a critical contribution, is the product of such pressures and responses. So too, unfortunately, may be increasing insecurity of employment, growing anxiety about the reliability of jobs and incomes, intensified pressures upon those in employment, and greater strains upon family life.

ENVIRONMENTAL PRESSURES

A breakneck pace of economic change and intensifying competition may also place the natural environment under increasing strain. Economic 'progress' has always posed a threat to the natural environment, with extensive deforestation, land despoliation and the extinction of species amongst the more obvious of consequences. The scale and manageability of such damage in the past has, however, been influenced by the relative (by contemporary standards) speed of economic and industrial changes that have generated the environmental challenges. The pace of contemporary change may, however, exceed the adjustment capacities of the environment and of many institutions and populations.

Accelerating deforestation in many of the world's tropical regions is one of the more obvious areas of contemporary environmental damage. More hidden, but no less pernicious in its effects, is the range of chemical pollution being inflicted upon the land, the sea and the air, with effects eventually appearing in the contamination or salination of land, the poisoning of seas and lakes, damage to the ozone layer of the atmosphere and general global warming. Resource consumption is also accelerating, whether the resource in question be agricultural land, water for irrigation and human consumption, or such critical commodities as oil.[31]

The scale and intensity of the resulting dislocations to environmental and human well-being could thus be one of the most pressing challenges facing the world at the start of the twenty-first century. Such dislocations could interact disastrously with a range of social and political disturbances. Political conflicts that spill over into armed conflict could add massively to the scale of damage inflicted by humanity upon the natural environment, as exemplified by the systematic burning of Kuwait's oil fields and the deliberate pollution of the waters of the Gulf by Iraq, during the war to liberate Kuwait from Iraqi occupation in 1991. However, political conflicts, with potentially violent consequences, could equally be prompted by growing environmental pressures. Oil resources were the subject of determined antagonisms amongst oil companies and their sponsoring governments for much of the first half of the twentieth century. Arguments over the use of water resources are well-established within the Middle-East. Disputes over access to deep-sea fishing grounds have already arisen between Britain and Iceland, between Spain and Canada, and have troubled relations within the European Community. Foreign polluters could arouse bitter antagonisms in the future and trigger serious counter-measures by those societies that are adversely affected.

SOCIAL BREAKDOWN

The net effect of a range of developments and dislocations that might be associated with further globalisation could be widespread social breakdown. In AICs, increasing unemployment amongst those with few skills, or in possession only of those skills that cannot readily be transferred to more promising areas of employment, will undercut the economic basis of the good life for many and foster the growth of an economic underclass. Where chronic unemployment is concentrated geographically it may, in turn, produce marginalised societies that are cut off physically and economically from the main-stream of the wider society.

However, the social damage of advancing globalisation may not be confined to those who are its most obvious victims. The pressures of rapid change and increasing insecurity of employment may impact upon a high proportion of the working population of AICs, to generate excess levels of stress, work-loads that cause family neglect, a focus on occupational demands that obstructs community concern and involvement and a general lapse into a fragile, short-term materialism. An excluded under-class and a neurotically insecure work-force might combine to generate high levels of social instability and potential turbulence, with potentially powerful political implications.[32]

The prospects for a number of the world's LDCs may, in many respects, be even worse than those for AICs subject to intensifying competitive pressures. A significant group of LDCs find themselves with patterns of economic specialisation, and with social and political institutions, that are poorly adapted for adjustment to, or certainly benefit from, many of the processes and pressures of globalisation. The primary commodities in which many LDCs are specialised are vulnerable to substantial price volatility. The exporting countries are thus, in turn, exposed to massive fluctuations in the income that they can earn from the world economy for the goods that they produce and export. The social and political systems of many such countries have also proven to be poorly equipped for the kind of rapid economic transformation, industrialisation and progress in export markets for manufactured goods, so spectacularly demonstrated by some of the NICs, particularly within South East Asia. In too many of the faltering LDCs, such weaknesses have been massively exacerbated by predatory behaviour like that of President Mobuto of Zaire, the self-destructive power struggles of Ghana or Sierra Leone, pernicious interference by external enemies like the former Apartheid regime of South Africa in

Angola and Mozambique or the protracted political insurgencies of a number of countries in Central America.

Societies that have failed thus far to develop developmental momentum may find it increasingly difficult to catch up with the 'express train' of the contemporary global economy. The consequences for a significant portion of the world which is progressively falling behind are many and worrying. Migration pressures might continue to grow to unmanageable proportions. Hostility towards the ever-more affluent parts of the world might increase to dangerous, and ultimately lethal, levels.

SOLUTIONS

The growing difficulties faced by the agencies of public governance remain a relatively abstract consequences of advancing globalisation for the bulk of the populations of most societies. Their direct experience is that of the accelerating pace of change in economic and industrial conditions and their subsequent social and environmental effects. Popular political reactions are spurred by such experiences and underlie a range of responses that governments may feel compelled to adopt in the future.

Trade with any one state or even group of countries is rarely the sole, or primary, cause of substantial changes in the conditions of workers in any given economy. There have, however, been some historical examples of the dramatic collapse of industries, such as that of the UK motor cycle industry in the face of Japanese imports, or the dislocations in Britain's agricultural industry with the repeal of the Corn Laws in the mid-nineteenth century and exposure to competition for overseas sources of grains.

The major source of job loss in today's AICs may well be the application of new production and information processing technologies. The ambient atmosphere of intensifying and accelerating international competitive pressures has, however, an important role in stimulating a concern to press ahead with the application of the latest technologies and 'lean' production processes amongst industrialists, and in encouraging a willingness amongst industrial and commercial workers to operate new technologies with smaller work forces.

The new global economy is also one in which economic growth proceeds remorselessly, with dramatic rates of growth exhibited (until recently at least) by the NICs. Environmental effects are compounded by such accelerating growth: resources are consumed more rapidly; pollution increases and spreads to regions that were previously spared. Conditions in some of the NICs are every bit as bad as they were in Europe's slum cities during its earlier phases of industrialisation. The effects of such growing environmental damage vary in their immediacy for those in different geographical locations, but they are palpable and pressing for many.

Whether real or rhetorical, the pressures of a globalising economy are frequently invoked in justification of employment practices that have increased part-time employment, increased the working hours of many sections of the population and stimulated a sense (albeit often exaggerated) of a new level of insecurity in employment. Unemployment levels in those of the AICs that have been reluctant to dissolve their painfully constructed welfare states or to promote infinitely 'flexible' labour markets have also risen substantially in the face of the competitive pressures, and technological possibilities, of the globalising economy.

One immediate effect of such developments is, as has been seen, the progressive marginalisation of an emergent 'underclass' which can now only expect protracted unemployment or employment in the most menial of jobs at the lowest possible wages.

The combined pressures of employment insecurities, depressive pressures on wage levels and the social ills attendant upon the persistence of an 'underclass' underlies the efforts that the governments of many countries still direct towards moderating such pressures and ameliorating their consequences. Unilaterally, governments of many countries still accompany a public commitment to the free-trade principles for the World Trade Organisation (WTO), with a wide range of measures of *de facto* economic protection and of promotion for their countries' industries and exports. Agricultural protection and promotion remains substantial within both the USA and the European Community, despite the commitments to substantial reform made during the completion of the Uruguay Round of negotiations under the General Agreement on Tariffs and Trade. The row between the European Community and the USA over the merger of Boeing with McDonnell Douglas[33] also reflected the intense commercial rivalry that persists between the two Unions and their respective firms and governments.

Education, training and the promotion of industrial innovation is also a major concern of governments in AICs and the NICs alike. A range of policies have been adopted in virtually all societies that seek international economic competitiveness to ensure ever-higher educational and technical standards amongst their young people, to increase the awareness of possibilities amongst their industrialists and to promote the development and application of technological innovations in industry and commerce. The problem here, however, is the difficulty of ensuring a growth of suitable jobs to meet any increase in the well-educated and technically competent work force.

At the collective level, governments have confined themselves to the promotion of as level a playing field as is possible for international trade and commerce, through such agencies as the WTO and new agreements on international financial rules and regulation. Little thought or attention has been paid at this level to the wider problem of securing a speed and scope of change in economic life that will prove manageable by human beings. The environment has begun to attract official concern, as witnessed by the succession of world summits on the environment. The measures adopted internationally to deal with such problems remain, however, relatively marginal to the core problems that persist and have been largely un-implemented by the large majority of signatory states.

While enhancing competitiveness remains a major objective of governments in a globalising world economy, they also have to deal with the casualties of, and losers from, the brave new world of accelerating global competition and technological change. Official responses range from the direct repression of the discontented dispossessed, as in many NICs, through to wide-ranging measures of social provision and support, as in many of the societies of North West Europe , including Scandinavia. Private responses range for charitable donations through to the creation of fenced housing compounds for the more affluent.

Recent enthusiasms within intellectual and political circles for ideas of economic *stakeholding*[34] or of political and social regeneration through communitarian principles and policies, reflect a concern with the kinds of economic dislocation that can be caused by intensifying economic competition and the socio-economic breakdown that may follow. Such doctrines may exert considerable appeal, enjoy short-term application, but are unlikely to resolve the underlying difficulties.

Ameliorative responses can clearly go some way towards dampening the impact of the more powerful effects of a globalising economy on individuals and groups. They may not, however, prove sufficient to calm the pressures that may arise within a number of AICs or do anything to stem the steady deterioration in the relative economic position of the majority of the LDCs. Within the AICs, resolution of the core problems thrown up by a globalising world require more vigorous solutions that address the economic marginalisation and social dislocation, and, ultimately, political disenfranchisement of the new 'underclass'. Growing internal disorder and conflict will be the fate of those industrial societies that fail their less fortunate members.

Within the majority of the LDCs, new approaches to economic and social development are required, but such approaches have thus far evaded easy identification. Continued failure to meet the developmental challenge will condemn such societies to continued, and probably growing, economic weakness, internal instability and external conflict.

The Green movement's advocacy of a return to a simpler, more localised, form of economic life offers one of the few systematic responses to the combined effects of remorseless economic growth, intensifying international economic competition and growing environmental pressure. The Green programme, however, contests the very basis of the prevailing economic system and would pose a fundamental challenge to what many of the inhabitants of the industrialised societies currently see as their basic rights and freedoms.[35] The popularity of the Green response to the contemporary economic condition is thus likely to remain seriously limited in the absence of clear and catastrophic environmental deterioration.

The collapse of effective public governance

Many of the sources and consequences of globalisation might thus fuse together to challenge effective public governance, in general, and the capabilities of state-level governments, in particular. Global financial integration has clearly reduced the degree to which state governments are the masters of their own financial fates. The spread of TNCs has weakened the capacities of state governments to control industrial and economic developments and, in particular, to extract desirable levels of taxation from the corporate sector. Reduced in the power to control or to secure adequate financial resources, state governments appear to be facing an unhappy future of constant, and ever-growing, demands with weakened capabilities for effective action.

If nature abhors a vacuum, this is no more true than in the area of politics and government. Calls for strong government tend to mount as weak governments falter in the face of increasing problems. Where effective government collapses into anarchy, new governing forces tend to arise within the society or to arrive from outside. The restoration of strong government is, however, rarely a gentle or democratic process and the resulting governments are rarely gentle or democratic. The external posture of such strong governments has often been hostile and/or assertive politically and, with some notable exceptions in the recent history of South East Asia and Latin America, mercantilist and/or protectionist externally. In the extreme case of a society collapsing, however, anarchy and severe economic disorder may be the long-lasting consequence.

Globalisation thus encompasses many of the central changes in the modern world. Substantial and rapid change is, and has always been, an unsettling and destabilising process.[36] Some of the solutions to the problems thrown up by advancing globalisation will arise more or less spontaneously, as for many of the great processes of change in history. Spontaneous solutions (such as mass starvation in the face of dislocations to food production and supply) are not, however, always happy solutions for significant parts of the populations experiencing them. The responsibility of governments and students of contemporary developments alike is to identify the sources and consequences of developments like globalisation with the greatest care and, where possible, plot the least painful paths towards the most effective patterns of response within and amongst the societies of the contemporary world.

Notes

1 For a further discussion of the contrasting 'strong', 'weak' and 'rejectionist' views of globalisation see: R.J. Barry Jones, *The World Turned Upside Down?: Globalisation and the Future of the State* (Manchester: Manchester University Press, 2000), chapter 1.

2 On which see: Richard O'Brien, *Global Financial Integration: The End of Geography* (London: RIIA/Pinter, 1992); and L. Bryan and D. Farrell, *Market Unbound: Unleashing Global Capitalism* (New York: J. Wiley, 1996).

3 Bryan and Farrell, *Market Unbound*, p. 34.

4 For a succinct discussion of which see: R.J. Barry Jones, *Conflict and Control in the World Economy: Contemporary Economic Realism and Neo-Mercantilism* (Brighton: Harvester/Wheatsheaf; Humanities Press in the USA, 1986), pp. 107–8.
5 P. Bailey, A. Parisotto and G. Renshaw (eds), *Multinationals and Employment: The Global Economy of the 1990s* (Geneva: International Labour Office, 1993), p. 8.
6 For an extreme view of which see: Manuel Castells, *The Rise of the Network Society* (Oxford: Blackwell, 1996).
7 For a wide-ranging discussion of the concept of world cities and its implications, see: P. Knox and P. Taylor (eds), *World Cities in a World-System* (Cambridge: Cambridge University Press, 1995).
8 For one view of the notion of global society and its prospects, see: Martin Shaw, *Global Society and International Relations: Sociological Concepts and Political Perspectives* (Cambridge: Polity Press, 1994).
9 For such an extreme view see: Kenichi Ohmae, *The End of the Nation-State: The Rise of Regional Economies* (New York: Free Press, 1995); but for criticisms of this view see: Linda Weiss, *The Myth of the Powerless State: Governing the Economy in a Global Era* (Cambridge: Polity Press, 1998); and for wide-ranging reviews see: Robert J. Holton, *Globalisation and the Nation State* (Houndmills: Macmillan, 1998); and Jones, *The World Turned Upside Down?*
10 See: John H. Dunning, *The Globalisation of Business* (London: Routledge, 1993).
11 For a summary of the foundations in Marxist political economy of such an interpretation see: M.C. Howard and J.E. King, *The Political Economy of Marx* (Harlow: Longman, 1975).
12 On the Gramscian approach see: S. Gill and D. Law, *The Global Political Economy: Perspectives, Problems and Policies* (London: Harvester/Wheatsheaf, 1988), chapters 5, 6 and 7.
13 See: S. Gill, 'Globalisation, market civilisation, and disciplinary neoliberalism', *Millennium: Journal of International Studies*, 24, 3 (Winter, 1995): 399–423.
14 For statements of the Realist view see: Robert Gilpin, *The Political Economy of International Relations* (Princeton, NJ: Princeton University Press, 1987); and Jones, *Conflict and Control in the World Economy*.
15 Raymond Vernon, *Sovereignty at Bay* (New York: Basic Books, 1971).
16 Robert Gilpin, *US Power and the Multinational Corporation: The Political Economy of Foreign Direct Investment* (New York: Macmillan, 1975).
17 For an overview of this problem see: Jones, *The World Turned Upside Down?*, esp. chapter 9.
18 For technical accounts of the formation of these institutions see: J.H. Richards, *International Economic Institutions* (London and New York: Holt Rinehart & Winston, 1970); and for general discussions of their role see: Evan Luard, *The Management of the World Economy* (London: Macmillan, 1983).
19 On which see: Jones, *Conflict and Control.*
20 See, especially, Susan Strange, *Casino Capitalism* (Manchester: Manchester University Press, 2nd edn, 1997), esp. chapter 2.
21 For interesting discussions of these and related issues see: Ian H. Rowlands, *The Politics of Global Atmospheric Change* (Manchester and New York: Manchester University Press, 1995).
22 For a review of many of these possibilities see: David Held, Anthony McGrew,

David Goldblatt and Jonathan Perraton, *Global Transformations* (Cambridge: Polity Press, 1999), chapter 7.
23 Dava Sobel, *Longitude* (London: Fourth Estate, 1996; published in the USA by Walker Publishing, 1995).
24 See: E. Braun and S. MacDonald, *Revolution in Miniature: The History and Impact of Semiconductor Electronics* (Cambridge: Cambridge University Press, 1978), esp. pp. 80–113.
25 For a wide-ranging discussion see: Susan Strange, *Mad Money* (Manchester: Manchester University Press, 1998).
26 For a brief account of derivatives see: Alison Watson, 'derivatives', in *The Routledge Encyclopaedia of International Political Economy* (London: Routledge, 2001).
27 For an authoritative survey of critical aspects of the problem see: Miles Kahler (ed.), *Capital Flows and Financial Crises* (Manchester: Manchester University Press, 1998).
28 On which see: Strange, *Mad Money*, chapter 9.
29 Face to face pressures from peers; value systems; 'side-payment's; or compulsion from governments or analogous authoritative agencies.
30 See: Jones, *Conflict and Control in the World Economy*, esp. chapters 6 and 7; Robert Wade, *Governing the Market: Theory and the Role of Government in East Asian Industrialisation* (Princeton, NJ: Princeton University Press, 1990); Linda Weiss and John M. Hobson, *States and Economic Development: A Comparative Historical Analysis* (Cambridge: Cambridge University Press, 1995); Ronen Palan and Jason Abbott (with Phil Deans), *State Strategies in the Global Political Economy* (London: Pinter, 1996); and Steve Chan, Cal Clark and Danny Lam, *Beyond the Developmental State* (Houndmills: Macmillan, 1998).
31 A concern that grew steadily throughout the latter decades of the twentieth century, *vide.* Committee on Resources and Man, *Resources and Man* (San Francisco: W.H. Freeman, 1969).
32 For a further discussion of these issues see: R.J. Barry Jones, 'Globalisation versus community', in Barry K. Gills (ed.), *Globalisation and the Politics of Resistance, New Political Economy*, 2, 1 (March, 1997): 39–51.
33 Report in *The Economist*, 'Brussels v Boeing', 19 July 1997, pp. 65–6.
34 On which see: Paul Ekins, *A New World Order: Grassroots Movements for Global Change* (London: Routledge, 1992), esp. p. 128.
35 See: A. Dobson, *Green Political Thought* (London: Unwin Hyman, 1990).
36 For a classic statement of such a processes and its problematical consequences, see: Karl Polanyi, *The Great Transformation: The Political and Economic Origins of Our Time* (Boston, MA: Beacon Press, 1957).

Further reading:

Bailey, P., Parisotto, A. and Renshaw, G., *Multinationals and Employment: The Global Economy of the 1990s* (Geneva: International Labour Office, 1993). A valuable survey of the effects of the growth and activity of multinational corporations upon patterns and prospects of employment.

Bryan, Lowell and Farrell, Diana, *Market Unbound: Unleashing Global Capitalism* (New

York: J. Wiley, 1996). An interesting discussion of the extent and effects of international financial integration.

Castells, Manuel, *The Informational City: Information Technology, Economic Restructuring, and the Urban-Regional Process* (Oxford: Basil Blackwell, 1989). A seminal account of the global consequences of the coming of the 'information age'.

Germain, Randall, *Globalisation and Its Critics* (London: Macmillan, 1997)

Gilpin, R., *US Power and the Multinational Corporation: The Political Economy of Foreign Direct Investment* (London: Macmillan, 1979). An early, but path-breaking, Realist view of multinational corporations and the international political economy.

Hoogvelt, Ankie, *Globalisation and the Post-Colonial World* (London: Macmillan, 1997). An invaluable review of the effects of globalisation upon the less developed countries.

Jones, R.J. Barry, 'Globalisation versus community', *New Political Economy,* 2, 1: 39–51. A succinct discussion of the implications of globalisation for social and economic cohesiveness.

Jones, R.J. Barry, *Globalisation and Interdependence in the International Political Economy: Rhetoric and Reality* (London: Pinter, 1995)

Jones, R.J. Barry, *Conflict and Control in the World Economy: Contemporary Economic Realism and Neo-Mercantilism* (Brighton: Harvester/Wheatsheaf, 1986). A wide-ranging review of economic Realist approaches to international economic relations.

Knox, P.L. and Taylor, P.J. (eds), *World Cities in a World System* (Cambridge: Cambridge University Press, 1995). An invaluable collection of papers on the 'world cities' concept.

O'Brien, R. *Global Financial Integration: The End of Geography* (London: RIIA/Pinter, 1992). An authoritative discussion of global financial integration.

6 Regionalisation within the contemporary world system

Patterns of contemporary regionalisation

The direction of contemporary developments is not unambiguously towards a fully integrated, increasingly homogenised, globalised system. Some prominent developments also point towards an increasingly regionalised world system, within which the previous tapestry of nation-states dissolve and give way to new economic, political and social configurations, which emerge to compete with one another on a still-fragmented world stage.[1]

The current picture of regionalisation is complex and its future path unclear. Two facets of regionalisation are prominent: political regionalisation and economic regionalisation. Moreover, the term region is employed with a variety of meanings, embracing: macro-regions, meso-regions and micro-regions.

Macro-regions are exemplified by the European Union, within which a number of sovereign states have come together to form a new, much larger entity. Meso-regions are generally smaller than macro-regions, but often transcend traditional state frontiers: Such meso-regions may formed by transborder areas of highly interconnected economic activity, such as the 'golden triangle' embracing parts of Germany, France and North Western Italy, or by patterns of cultural or ethnic identify, such as the Basque region of Northern Spain and South Western France.[2] Micro-regions, finally, are usually smaller territorial areas within established states, which exhibit a high degree of economic interconnection – such as the Thames corridor in the UK – or cultural or ethnic identity.

Much of the debate about regionalisation on the world stage has been devoted to the prospects and impact of macro-regions. Here, the political and economic dimensions of regionalisation have often been inter-related but often exhibit differences in pace and direction of development. Thus, the deep interconnection between political and economic developments within Western Europe since the Second World War has not been replicated elsewhere.

Forms of regionalisation

- Macro-regions: large conglomerations of states and/or other formerly distinct economies
- Meso-regions: smaller than macro-regions, but embracing elements of separate states or formerly distinct economies
- Micro-regions: small areas of economic life within states (or former states)

The European Union – the troubled fusion of political and economic regional integration

Western Europe has emerged as the model for successful regional integration in the contemporary international system and as the major source of expectations of a regionalising world. [3] The theories that seek to explain this development are both varied and highly controversial, as will be seen in the section on the sources of regionalisation. The post-war record does, however, describe a process of progressive integration politically and economically.

The political regionalisation of Western Europe

Political purposes underlay the early moves towards regional integration within post-war Europe. The formation of the European Coal and Steel Community (ECSC) in 1952 was the direct product of beliefs that the integration of the production and distribution of coal and steel under a common high authority, and answerable to a parliament and a Court of Justice, was one of the best ways to ensure against the renewal of armed conflict within Western Europe. It was felt particularly important to bring the coal and steel production of Germany and France under common control.[4]

Success with the Coal and Steel Community encouraged further movement towards the creation of a wider-ranging community within Western Europe. The Messina Conference of June 1955 was devoted to negotiating the basis of a new European Economic Community, with the ultimate purpose of fostering political harmony, and ultimate integration, amongst the states of Western Europe. Protracted negotiations eventually resulted in the signature of the Treaty of Rome, which established the European Economic Community (EEC) and the European Atomic Energy Community (EURATOM), both of which came into formal existence on 1 January 1958 and both of which had similar institutions to those of the European Coal and Steel Community.

The early progress towards integration within Western Europe was not, however, clear and consistent. Attempts to create a European Defence Community (EDC) in the early 1950s foundered in the face of rising doubts about its desirability and likely effectiveness. The North Atlantic Treaty Organization (NATO), with the pivotal membership of the United States of America, thus remained the only functioning instrument for the collective defence in Europe and the North Atlantic area. Moreover, the original European Economic Community embraced only six of the countries of Western Europe: France, Germany, Italy, Belgium, the Netherlands and Luxembourg.

Integration within the Western European region did, however, continue to deepen and widen. The agencies of the ECSC, the EEC and EURATOM were fused in 1965, to form one Council of Ministers, the new European Commission, and a single European Court of Justice. Widening then followed with the successive accessions to the EEC of Britain, Ireland and Denmark in 1973, Greece in 1981 and Spain in 1986. A protracted period of stagnation in institutional development was then broken in the mid 1980s with the negotiation of the Single European Act, a measure designed primarily to introduce a totally integrated market for goods and services throughout the EEC, but also involving the introduction of the principle of (qualified) majority voting within the governing Council of Misters over a wide range of policy issues related to the introduction of the integrated market.

The momentum given to integration by the Single European Act was then carried on into the negotiation of the Maastricht Treaty of 1993 which formally established the European Union upon three 'pillars', the economic European Community; the intention to develop a Common Foreign and Security Policy; and the principles and practices of common citizenship. The Maastricht Treaty clarified the ambitions for political integration within Western Europe that had been entertained by many of the founding fathers, and subsequent enthusiasts, of the European Economic Community in the 1950s. It also established a time-table for the future monetary integration within the European Union and the adoption of a common currency (from which the UK and Denmark both secured 'opt out' agreements). The Maastricht Treaty, however, also precipitated some of the most marked opposition to further integration amongst the populations of

Western European countries.[5] Referenda on the ratification of the Treaty produced only the barest of a majority for ratification in France and a marginal, yet highly significant, initial defeat in Denmark.[6] Policies adopted within many of the EU's member states subsequently, designed to generate economic conditions that satisfied the Maastricht Treaty's criteria for participation in Economic and Monetary Union also produced considerable trouble, as popular opposition developed in response to a range of increasingly desperate efforts to meet the 'convergence' criteria for membership of the monetary union, including reduced budgets for public services and a range of measures of financial restraint.[7]

A further expansion of membership of the European Union also took place during the era of the Maastricht Treaty. The remaining members of the European Free Trade Area (EFTA) (a looser, free-trade association of those European states that had not joined the European Economic Community) began to turn with increasing interest towards the EU. A European Economic Area was the first product of this new interest. It gave the EFTA members – Austria, Finland, Norway and Sweden full rights of access to the markets of the European Union, but not participation in its decision-making institutions.[8] The terms of full membership were then negotiated. However, a referendum on membership of the EU in Norway was defeated decisively; a referendum in Sweden produce a clear, but modest, majority in favour of joining. At the start of 1995, Austria, Finland and Sweden acceded to the European Union. By the end of the decade, negotiations were underway on future membership of the EU by Cyprus, Malta, the Czech Republic, Hungary and Poland, with considerable interest also being expressed by other Central and Eastern European countries and by the new Balkan states of Slovenia and Croatia.

The economic regionalisation of Western Europe

Growing regionalisation within Western Europe has accompanied the fitful progress towards political integration. The most decisive evidence for economic regionalisation is provided by the levels of trade that members of the European Community undertake within one another (intra-regional trade), when compared with trade with the wider world. Between 1975 and 1990 such intra-regional trade, within the then twelve member states of the European Community, had risen from 52.5 per cent to 60.7 per cent of total trade. The significance of this level of intra-regional trade is highlighted by the fact that, in 1989, the twelve members of the European Community were responsible for only 27 per cent of world wealth creation (GDP) and should, therefore, have been expected to attract only a comparable level of the trade from its own members.

The European Community also acts as a major pole of attraction for the exports of the economies of its neighbours by land or across the Mediterranean. In 1989 70.6 per cent of Algeria's exports were sent to the EC in 1989, 54.7 per cent of Cyprus's, and 75.8 per cent of Malta's. In 1990 45.7 per cent of the exports of the former Yugoslavia were directed towards the then European Community of 12 states, 77.8 per cent of Tunisia's and 53.2 per cent of Turkey's.[9]

The dramatic levels of intra-regional trade within the European Community reflect a number of the influences that will be discussed in the section on 'sources', particularly geographical proximity and the industrialised character of the leading members of the Community. The effects of clear political commitments to foster economic integration have, however, played a decisive role and been at the heart of the institutional basis of progressive integration: the European Coal and Steel Community; the original European Economic Community, with its common external tariffs and Common Agricultural Policy; the Single European Act, and its promotion of a fully integrated market; and the Maastricht Treaty.

The impressive level of intra-regional trade within the European Community has not, however, yet secured the full convergence of the economies of its member states. Many structural features of the economies of the expanded European Union differ markedly. At the end of 1994 the wealth (GDP per capita) of the members of the European Union, varied sharply, from $309,833 per year per person in Luxembourg down to $7,705 per person per year in Greece.[10] Moreover, the degree to which the different economies of the European Union are linked, and sensitive, to one another varies considerably. Correlations of growth rates between 1986 and 1996 varied from a quite strong +0.52 between France and Germany to a weakly negative –0.2 between Germany and the UK.[11] Indeed, it is the persistence of such structural diversity and lack of syncronicity that poses the greatest challenge to the project for Economic and Monetary Union within the European Union.

Regionalism beyond Europe

There have also been signs of growing regionalisation across the American Continent and within South East Asia. Both processes have economic and political facets.

THE AMERICAS[12]

The economy of the United States of America has exerted a strong, albeit uneven, influence upon all the other economies on the American Continent for many years. The closer that another economy has been geographically the greater, in general, has been the proportion of its exports that have been directed towards the USA. By the end of 1994, 81.7 per cent of Canada's exports went to the USA and 84.9 per cent of Mexico's.[13] This force of attraction has, moreover, gradually redirected the trade of some (but not all) of the economies that were formerly members of European empires away from their former colonial masters and towards the USA. Between 1970 and 1989 Bermuda's exports to the USA rose from 10.5 per cent of total exports to 34.4 dollars and those of St. Kitts and Nevis rose from 1.7 per cent to 50.3 per cent. Jamaica, in contrast sent 61 per cent of its exports to the USA in 1970 and only 49.6 per cent in 1989.[14] Moreover, the USA's exports have not been concentrating markedly upon its continental neighbours: sending 20.7 per cent to Canada in 1970 and 20.9 per cent in 1990; with 15.2 per cent sent to the other Continental economies in 1970 and only 13.8 per cent in 1990.[15]

The strategic salience of the entire continent to the United States of America, and the importance of the US economy to many of its continental neighbours, motivates interest in an eventual Free Trade Area of the Americas. This, however, is an aspiration that remains beset with complications and obstacles,

Such uneven trends towards economic regionalisation have been accompanied by a number of initiatives at the political level to foster regional economic association. The North American Free Trade Area (NAFTA), embracing the USA, Canada and Mexico is the most prominent of these initiatives and seeks to consolidate, and regulate, a region of economic interaction that was already of major significance to Canada and Mexico. Elsewhere on the American Continent there have also been a number of attempts to form regional economic associations over the years. Many of the past ventures in this direction have met with little, or no, success. Recent initiatives have, however, been more substantial in their effects. MERCOSUR, at the southern end of the Continent, has created a free-trade area amongst Argentina, Brazil, Uruguay and Paraguay and a substantial growth of intra-regional trade and productive specialisation, which has subsequently attracted associated agreements from Chile and Bolivia. The Andean Pact soon split into two sub-groups: Colombia, Venezuela and Ecuador; and Peru and Bolivia. The members of the Central American Common Market (CACM) of Nicaragua, El Salvador, Cost Rica, Honduras and Guatemala continue to be closely associated with the US economy and are sufficiently concerned about the effects of the NAFTA to seek a comparable agreement with the USA for themselves. The Caribbean Common Market (CARICOM) has, with the USA's support, sought to promote intra-regional trade, development and environmental protection.

REGIONALISM IN SOUTH EAST AND EAST ASIA

South East Asia has also exhibited tendencies towards regionalisation: under both economic and political influences.[16] Economically, South East and East Asia has been an area of spectacular economic growth and development during the 1980s and 1990s. This has stimulated cross-border investments by the firms of South East Asian countries, and particularly by Japan. However, the motor force for much of the development within South East Asia has been the growing opportunities for exports to the markets of the richer (largely Western) parts of the world.[17] Such export dependence upon the 'West' has generated unease about the ultimate reliability of such export markets and a growing concern to develop more local markets for the expanding industrial output of the South East Asian 'tiger' economies. The promotion of regional integration, and of mutually supportive patterns of economic development and production, has thus been a conscious policy response of South East Asian elites to the imbalanced trade relationship between the region and the advanced industrial 'West'; and the development of the Association of Sea East Asian countries (ASEAN), its institutional expression.

On the economic front, the objectives of ASEAN have, thus far, been limited to the promotion of the reduction of the tariffs that South East Asian economies apply to imports from other South East Asian economies. The objective has thus been limited to the development of a modest free-trade area rather than a more ambitious structure of formal regional economic integration. Even in its modest pursuit of a free-trade area however, ASEAN has made only limited progress thus far. Moreover, the formation of the Asia-Pacific Economic Cooperation forum (APEC) has complicated the regional character of South East Asia by drawing its members into a wider association that includes, and has often been promoted by, the non-regional United States of America.

Intra-regional trade has however increased modestly within South East Asia, despite the persistence of many formal and informal restraints. Between 1970 and 1990, the proportion of exports sent to other South East Asian economies increased: from 6.3 per cent to 14 per cent in the case of Hong Kong, from 20.7 per cent to 24.6 per cent for Indonesia, from 7 per cent to 17.3 per cent for South Korea, from 31.8 per cent to 38.7 per cent for Malaysia, from 7.2 per cent to 19.1 per cent for the Philippines, and from 13.2 per cent to 40.2 per cent in the case of Singapore. Only Thailand amongst the 'young tigers' showed a decline in the proportion of exports being sent to other South East Asian economies: from 30.7 per cent in 1970 to 20.8 per cent in 1990.[18] By 1994 it was estimated that about half of the exports of 'developing' Asia's exports went to other Asian economies, with some 37 per cent going to other 'developing' Asian economies.

Security and political issues within the South East Asian region have also been the focus of the ASEAN Regional Forum (ARF). This has sought to deal with a wide range of contentious, and potentially dangerous, issues ranging from territorial disputes between mainland China and her regional neighbours,[19] through to the degree to which Western-style democracy and human rights' issues ought to be embraced within the region. Again, however, ARF remains limited in its objectives[20] and has, thus far, exhibited no ambitions towards regional political integration.

REGIONALISATION WITHIN THE MIDDLE EAST

The Middle East paints a highly contradictory image from the point of view of regionalism.[21] Whilst the call for Arab unity and the idea of Pan-Arabism has always been at the forefront of the politics of the Middle East, Arab regimes have been more pre-occupied with ensuring their own political survival. What marks the Middle East from other regions in the international system is the number of long-standing inter-state and intra-state conflicts. As such, the formation of regional organisations has been motivated by the existing or potential dangers to the security of regimes.

The most well-known regional organisation is the Arab League. Set up in 1945, it membership includes all the Arab states. The existence of the Arab League is meant to reflect the goals of Arab nationalism, namely the breaking down of regional divisions in the Arab world and the establishment of a single Arab state. In reality, it is an organisation of independent sovereign states each with their own separate conceptions of national interest. Although it serves as a forum for discussion amongst Arab states, it has failed to make significant impact on issues of major importance. Rather than serving as a unifying body, it has been an arena where battles between different regimes have been fought out and where governments have sought to pursue their own interests and enhance their own security, often at the expense of others. In the 1950s and 1960s, the League was divided between self-styled radical regimes and those which were seen as conservative. In the 1970s and 1980s the League was split over the differing approaches towards resolving the Arab–Israeli conflict and the Palestinian question.

The Middle East is a peculiar exception to the overall emerging trend towards regional economic cooperation. The Middle East is not only the least integrated region in the world economy but it is also characterised by the lowest degree of regional economic cooperation. The level of intra-Arab trade between countries accounts for less than 5 per cent of external trade of the region. The Middle East has failed to benefit from the global trends towards economic and political liberalisation. The state still remains heavily involved in the management of the economies. Dictatorial regimes, inefficient and corrupt bureaucratic stuctures and the absence of a flourishing private sector have proved to be significant barriers to the development of private domestic and foreign investment in the region. Governments have been resistant to the development of civil society in the fear that economic and political liberalisation might unleash forces for reform and change which they would be unable to control.

The absence of a stable security environment and the lack of economic development should serve as a motivation for greater regional cooperation. However, the existing political and economic structures of Arab states, the lack of complementarity between their economies and the resistance towards taking significant steps towards economic and political liberalisation all suggest that the prospects for regionalism in the Middle East are low. Whilst limited moves towards more economic cooperation are indeed possible, it is not realistic to expect the development of new cooperative structures or the emergence of schemes for Middle East wide regional integration modelled on the European or NAFTA models

REGIONALISATION WITHIN AFRICA

Africa is often thought to be an area in which regionalisation has been a notable failure. Explicit efforts to create free trade areas have often been frustrated, not least by the impact of political instability in participating countries. Moreover, the effects of past imperial control, and the continuing influence of the poles of economic attraction within the advanced industrial countries, are thought to bias the export trade of African economies towards the richer economies of the 'West'.

The actual situation within Africa is, however, a little more complicated than is often supposed. Political instability has certainly disrupted many integrative initiatives. However, the Organisation of African Unity (OAU) has a well-established secretariat, and a long track record of regular meetings. A number of West African states have also sought to restore political stability in neighbouring societies under the banner of the Economic Community of West African States (ECOWAS). Moreover, the export trade of African economies reveals considerable variability: with exports to other African economies ranging (in 1989) from 1.1 per cent for Liberia to 54.7 per cent for Chad.[22] In general, it is the low levels of income and wealth – a mere 2 per cent of World GDP for the whole of Africa; and 1 per cent of World GDP for Sub-Saharan Africa, in 1989 – that are the main reasons for low levels of exports amongst African countries. Indeed, the overall level of intra-regional trade within Africa actually exceeds by some 2.4 times what would be expected from the relative wealth (in world terms) of the importing countries.[23] Regionalisation within Africa, and within some sub-regions in particular, might thus progress rapidly were the growth of wealth and income to accelerate within the continent.

REGIONALISATION WITHIN THE FORMER SOVIET UNION AND EASTERN AND CENTRAL EUROPE

One of the major effects of the 'end of the Cold War' and the dissolution of the former Soviet Union has been the rapid reversal of what was previously a high level of economic integration and political control amongst the constituent states of the Soviet Union itself, and its subordinate territories in Central and Eastern Europe. Intra-regional trade amongst the members of the Council for Mutual Economic Aid (CMEA) (otherwise known as COMECON) was high before the fall of the Berlin Wall – 62.3 per cent in 1960 and 53.7 per cent in 1985 – and dropped markedly thereafter – to a mere 38.2 per cent by 1990 – as the Soviet Unions former satellites sought to reorientate their trade towards the wider world economy and, in particular, towards Western Europe.[24]

The diversity and fragmentation that arose from the ashes of the Soviet Empire may not, however, persist indefinitely. Within the former Soviet Union, efforts have been made to restore some measure of economic and political association: measures that have ranged from savage conflict in the Chechen Republic to the deployment of a range of economic inducements in the case of less turbulent neighbours. Many of the Soviet Union's former satellites in Central and Eastern Europe have, in contrast, shown increasing enthusiasm for another arena of regionalisation – that within Western Europe – and have formed a queue of potential members of the European Union.

A world of meso and micro-regions?

Macro-regions have often appeared to be the primary concern of policy-makers and analysts, with their interests in regional integration, regional security structures and other arrangements involving the established states of differentiable regions of the world system. The potentialities of meso-regions and micro-regions have, however, begun to attract growing concern in recent years, but pose a potentially serious threat to the established states and the larger regional organisations in which their decision-makers have often sought to involve themselves.

Some potential meso-regions reflect cultural and/or ethnic identities that overlap conventional state borders. Where there is such dissonance between established state frontiers and more 'natural' patterns of affiliation, the authority and capability of the state has often been directed to the suppression of a potential meso-region that might threaten to force substantial reconfigurations of political boundaries and jurisdictions. Comparable problems have arisen with micro-regions based upon cultural or ethnic identities that differ from that, or those, of the majority within an established state.

The economic bases of meso-regionalism or micro-regionalism have also attracted increasing attention within recent years. This has been stimulated by considerations of the effects both of growing economic integration within macro-regions, like the European Community, and of globalisation. A 'golden triangle' that crosses the mutual borders of Germany, France and Italy appears to have arisen within Western Europe. A 'golden triangle' of a rather more sinister variety has long been established in the border region amongst Burma, China, Laos, Thailand and Vietnam within which extensive opium cultivation underpins the production of a substantial portion of the world's illicit heroin supply.

The distinction between meso-regions and micro-regions is largely a matter of size (in terms of area and population encompassed) and scope (in terms of the elements of the otherwise separate societies involved). Culture and identity also play a part, although their role varies considerably from one context to another. In some cases, differences of culture and identity are the fundamental criteria of micro-regions; in other cases, economic characteristics may mark out a micro-region that embraces considerable cultural variations and differing identities. Thus Kenichi Ohmae identifies one such emergent region within the world economy as that of San Diego in the USA, Tijuana in Mexico, Hong Kong and Southern China – a meso-region of substantial size and cultural diversity. He also identifies Research Triangle Park in North Carolina, USA, as an emergent region – clearly a micro-region of relatively small size and substantial cultural homogeneity.[25]

To a considerable extent, meso- and micro-regions identified in terms of patterns of economic life relate to Robert Scalapino's notion of 'natural economic territories'. However, the operability of such a notion may be challenged by the complexity of patterns of economic activity and association in practice. Patterns exhibited in one sphere of economic life may not always be identical with those revealed in some other area. 'Regions' may thus be differently identified according to the economic (or other) activities that are defined as central.

Regionalisation is thus a complex feature of the contemporary world scene. Beliefs that the world is fragmenting into distinct, and mutually competitive, regions are qualified by the ambiguous evidence of the progress of such regionalisation in practice. Only Western Europe shows clear evidence of progressive regionalisation, and even this is challenged by the emergence of opposition to further integration, politically and economically, and by the persistence of many, important links between Western European societies and those outside the region.

The pattern of regionalisation is also an uncertain matter. Trends towards macro-regionalisation are, themselves, complicated, and partly challenged, by contrasting tendencies towards meso- and micro-regionalisation. The patterns of meso- and micro-regionalisation are also highly variable. Some are directed by political and/or cultural considerations; others are driven by economic developments. Economic patterns of meso- and micro-regionalisation may, moreover, vary according to the areas of economic life that are determining developments.

The sources of contemporary regionalisation

The earlier discussion of patterns of regionalisation within the international system indicated the complexity of contemporary developments. The strength of macro-regions vary considerably. Moreover, the simple picture of a world of a few macro-regions is considerably complicated by the simultaneous patchwork of meso-regions. Micro-regions can also be discerned within the states that compose macro-regions and within the meso-regions that have developed at a number of cross-border foci of economic activity.

The definition and identification of the regions that contribute to the contemporary world scene is closely associated with questions about the driving forces of such regionalisation. The major distinction, here, is between extrinsic definitions of regions and intrinsic definitions: a dichotomy that is obliquely related to the division between the shaping of the emergence and functioning of regions by forces that are external to them and those that are internal.

The definition of regions

Extrinsic criteria of regions and their existence are those established by observers of any region, whether they are members of communities not included within the region in question or detached analysts. The existence of a region by such criteria is thus a matter of ascription on the basis of what appears to be the case to the outsider and/or some explicit theory of why and where regions should be expected to emerge.

Intrinsic criteria of regions are more to do with the perceptions and perspectives of those who are engaged in developing or maintaining regions. Popular feelings of common identity would be one such criterion. The ambitions of those who seek to construct some new regional focus for economic, political and social life, would constitute another form of intrinsic criterion of a region.

Extrinsic and Intrinsic criteria of regions are both heavily dependent upon the existing ideas of those who observe or promote regions: theoretical ideas about the role of regions within the developing international political economy and/or political doctrines about desirable patterns of future political, economic and social association.

The causes of regionalisation

The contrasting criteria of regions are obliquely related to differing views about the basic forces driving current processes of regionalisation. Here, an emphasis upon the influence of external forces in growing regionalisation contrasts sharply with stress upon the internal sources of cohesive regions. External forces for regionalisation focus upon the growing competition within the international political economy, the range of difficulties created by the advance of globalisation and the uncertainties generated by the end of the Cold War and the birth of a 'new world disorder'. The growing scale and speed of competitive pressures within the international economy, it is argued, have made it increasingly difficult for firms that continue to operate exclusively within one national economy to retain competitiveness. Within a new regional economy, firms can exploit larger markets, and combine their efforts and/or amalgamate into larger, more competitive units, to confront international competitors more effectively. The efforts of regional governments can also be combined to provide powerful support for 'regional champions'. The financial support of entire regions can be mobilised behind new industrial developments; region-wide schemes for innovation and technical improvement can be put in place; and, where necessary, a large, sheltered market can be provided for new products during the early phases of their development and marketing.

Advancing globalisation also creates pressures for regionalisation. Globalisation creates new problems for effective governance. New forms of global governance, it is thought, are confronted by the problems of scale, cultural diversity, and widespread failures of compliance by recalcitrant governments. Vigorous regional authorities, in contrast, can operate on a more modest scale, with contributing states that are more alike in their institutions and aspirations, and may be more effective in securing consistent compliance with any regulative efforts.

The post-Cold War 'new world disorder' has also brought new dangers. With the removal of the world-wide control of the USA and the USSR, old frictions have re-emerged and new conflicts been spawned. Economic and environmental pressures have also been making themselves felt with force in a number of areas of potential political instability. The volatile mixture of weakened control and new sources of instability and conflict has created a world which poses threats that are distinct from those of the era of the Cold War. New regional associations may help in such circumstances in two ways: first, by providing the basis of new regional security arrangements for protection against external threats; and, second, by creating new mechanisms for preserving stability, and resolving potential conflicts, within regions that may be prone to potential eruptions.

The primary forces for more regionalisation may not, however, be located exclusively in the world outside each region. A range of internal forces and ambitions may also drive regionalisation. At the social, cultural and political level, a popular sense of common identity could prompt moves towards regional association. However, such sentiments have rarely arisen spontaneously and have more often been the result of new thinking amongst political elites and opinion formers. Leading considerations for such advocates of regionalisation have been a history of damaging conflicts amongst the members societies of the potential region and/or a sense that current political divisions are artificial and, ultimately, unhelpful to political and economic development. Much of the post–1945 enthusiasm for European regional integration was directed by a profound reaction against the experience of Europe's embroilment in two major conflagrations within the past thirty years. The future peace and prosperity of Europe lay, for such advocates, in the combined effects of integrating Europe's economies within a new, regional economy and its management through new, region-wide institutions of governance.

Periodic enthusiasm amongst political leaders for regional integration within sub-Saharan Africa reflects a feeling that the current political complexion of the area is more a function of past colonial control than any 'natural' divisions. Within parts of North Africa and the Middle East occasional efforts towards integration have been prompted by doctrines of pan-Arabism and/or a common Islamic faith and culture.

Internal forces for regionalisation are not exclusively political or cultural in their origins however. Economic interests may also exert a profound influence in favour of regional economic integration. Within the European Community, the prospects of larger markets and reduced transaction costs of many forms, have persuaded large financial, commercial and manufacturing interests to exert a continuing influence in favour of regional integration and its further development.

Internal forces for greater regional integration are rarely unopposed, however. Political and cultural currents in favour of integration invariably prompt a reaction through the reassertion of valuable local traditions and identities which, it is held, will be diluted, and possibly dissolved, by the further advance of regionalisation. Economic interests are equally not all in favour of regional economic integration. Smaller enterprizes have often anticipated fewer opportunities from regional economic integration and have, in sharp contrast, perceived the danger of new competitors entering their traditional markets from the other member economies of any new regional economy.

Organised labour has often been equally suspicious of moves towards regional economic integration.[26] Increased competition from firms operating in economies with lower wage levels, and with less rigorous conditions of employment and production, have been perceived to carry serious risk of job losses within firms in higher-wage/higher-standards economies. Even where jobs are not actually to be lost, there is a fear that severe downward pressures will be exerted upon the wages and conditions of work of those employed in the more advanced economies within any new regional economy.

The processes of regional integration

The discussion of sources opens up the issue of whether the process of regionalisation is the result of automatic pressure or has to be directed by interested human beings. The Functionalist theory of regional integration emphasises the general pressure for greater integration that is exerted by developments within economic, environmental or technical arenas.[27] The need for greater integration in institutions, decision-making systems and political structure is thus driven by 'needs' generated in these more material spheres. Participants in institutional and political life gradually come to appreciate the requirements for integrative changes in their arenas of activity as pressing problems and requirements become ever-more clear. The Functionalist dynamic is, moreover, cumulative, with requirements generated in one area stimulating new needs elsewhere; and with institutional changes in one domain prompting changes in others. The requirements for more effective management of a region's natural environment might thus prompt the emergence of new, and more effective, institutions for regional environmental governance. New political institutions for environmental management should, in turn, generate new laws and regulations which require adapted, or even wholly new, legal institutions to administer.

The relative impersonality, and automaticity, of such a Functionalist view of the integration process does not, however, find favour with those who are more impressed by the uneven experiences of past experiments with regional integration. One response to this mixed picture has been the development of a Neo-Functionalist approach, which emphasises the pivotal role of political authorities and interests in driving forward integration at critical junctures, in addition to the spill-over effects from one area of integration to another.[28]

Other theorists of integration, however, give clear primacy to the prior role of political authorities and their political aspirations. To such analysts, no substantial progress towards integration can be made without the prior commitment of such authorities to the creation of a framework that is suitable for the growth of economic interactions, social associations and other forms of relationship of

Theoretical views of regional integration

- Federalist: integration requires the prior commitment of elites to the principle and institutions of integration
- Functionalist: integration will follow from pressures (mainly economic) for supra-national forms of government
- Neo-functionalist: Functionalist dynamics can operate, but only with judicious intervention by appropriate political authorities and a good measure of 'spill over' amongst different issue areas
- Inter-governmentalist: integration only takes place when it suits national governments and continues for so long, and in such forms, as suit the developing interests of national governments

endurance and wide scope. Peace is thus a precondition for extensive economic integration within any geographical area. Stable and reliable rules and regulations are, again, a prior necessity for complex and enduring economic relationships. Such notions lay at the heart of the views of Federalists, who sought to build the integration of Western Europe from the commitments of a cohort of post-war political leaders to the principles and practices of a new federal polity for the region.[29]

The motives for regionalisation

The intentional creation of an integrated region will, however, be substantially influenced by the primary motives of the main actors. The range of motives for regionalisation is considerable: from peace, economic strength and regional well-being, ethnic or cultural reintegration, through to supposed progress towards world-wide prosperity and well-being

Differentiating neatly between political and economic motives in human conduct is not always a simple task, but is necessary when considering regionalisation, its complications and potential pitfalls. The need for such differentiation is to allow any possible incompatibilities between political and economic purposes or practices to be identified and their implications reviewed.

The European Union exemplifies a case of regionalisation in which both political and economic motives have played a prominent part. Politically, advocates of greater European integration have aspired to a new European polity, with a capacity for regional governance on something between a confederal and fully federal basis. Central to the development of a new European polity has been the development of a new popular sense of European political identity. The creation of the European Parliament was explicitly directed to such an end. The political integration of Western Europe can, however, be seen to have two distinguishable objectives: the purely political purpose of a new political community within which war will become unthinkable; and the creation of a new political institution capable of shaping a dynamic and more powerful European economy within an increasingly competitive world economy.

An enhanced European economy is, however, an objective that does not entail the creation of a distinctive new European polity. Free-market approaches towards economic improvement require little more of Europe than the establishment of a genuinely free-trade area, in which state-based obstacles to the operations of enterprises are removed: a project requiring the removal of formal trade barriers and those other rules and regulations that unduly differentiate the markets of previously distinct economies.

The practical complexities of distinguishing the motives and processes of regionalisation are, however, demonstrated by the case of Economic and Monetary Union (EMU) within the European Union: the 'common currency' project. The problem here is whether the purpose of EMU is actually primarily political or economic. Many observers of EMU contend that the real motive is political: the establishment of the new common currency which will both require a new quasi-government to cover all the member societies of the new monetary community and which will provide that government with its clearest symbol of economic sovereignty. Other views of EMU, however, emphasise the argument that it is actually a necessary condition for a genuinely free-trade area within the European Union, in which all costly barriers (including the financial costs of trading across different currencies) have been removed. Political and economic purposes may thus both be evident in arguments for European Economic and Monetary Union and their practical implications inextricably intertwined in practice.

Pan-Arabism has been fuelled by adherence to a common religion – Islam – the use of a common, formal Arabic language by educated elites, and, in some member states, a sense of a shared Arab ethnicity. Such a sense of commonality complements other economic and political motives for regional association and possible integration. It has not, thus far however, succeeded in overcoming the substantial institutional obstacles that inhibited enduring integration amongst the distinct states of the region.

Ethnic, cultural and religious motives for regionalisation have been evident within the Middle East and North Africa. Clear political and economic purposes, including the confrontation with Israel, were attached to intended associations like the short-lived United Arab Republic between Egypt and Syria and the proposed link between Egypt and Libya, but commonalities of background and experience remained a primary foundation.

Regionalisation has also, on occasions, been heralded as a positive contribution towards greater global integration and harmony. The argument here is a little more complicated than in the case of many other motives for regionalisation, for regionalisation carries, as will be seen later, a threat of fragmenting the global system into mutually hostile blocks.

Regionalisation might not lead to divisiveness, however, if successful regionalisation were to establish experience of effective integrative processes and demonstrate the general advantages of the coming together of formerly sovereign political and economic societies. A successfully integrated region would thus become a clear stepping-stone on the climb to a fully integrated global system in which formal barriers amongst peoples had been abolished, new institutions of effective global governance created, and a new sense of common identify fomented.

The major motors of regionalisation

Discussions of regionalisation also follow the debates about globalisation in emphasising the potency of a few factors and forces in driving the process forward. Two such sets of factors and forces stand out: the economic pressures of an increasingly globalised and competitive world economy, and both the pressure and possibilities created by a range of new technologies of information processing and of manufacture.

The pressures of an increasingly competitive international economy are, as has suggested previously, often cited in favour of a conscious move to greater regionalisation. Two features of this argument are worth highlighting. The first is the contention that single-state economies no longer provide a sufficient basis for effective economic activity within the world economy that has emerged. The governments of individual states are now thought to be incapable, when acting alone, of maintaining effective influence over those aspects of economic developments that bear directly upon the effectiveness of their policies or the well-being of their populations. Collaborative efforts on a regional basis are thus held to offer the best, indeed only, feasible path to the effective moderation of the effects of the new global economy and to preserving an ability to promote general well-being.

The economies of scale being exploited by the world's leading firms are now also thought to be such as to necessitate new responses, particularly by new regionally based enterprizes that are able to benefit from region-wide 'home' markets, exploit all the productive strengths of the regions societies and secure the large-scale support of regional authorities. Regional authorities can support such responses by reducing the intra-regional obstacles faced by firms and by providing positive support, including the development and application of expensive technologies. The European Union's support, both direct and indirect, for the Airbus consortium, in its struggle with Boeing for the world-wide market for larger commercial aircraft,[30] exemplifies such an approach to, and rationale for, regionalisation.

The impact of the new technologies of information gathering, processing and distribution reinforce the general pressures for regionalisation exerted by the intensification of economic competition within the world economy. Here regional authorities can, again, play both a direct and indirect role. A regional authority will be able to assist the vitality of information technology enterprizes, and the emergence of suitable markets, with a range of direct measures, including training programmes, grants for research and development and procurement programmes. Indirectly, regional authorities can also exert an influence on the general regulation of the new 'wired world' by virtue of their size and, therefore, command over critical segments of the world's market for information technology products and services. Big may, in short, be beautiful when it comes to negotiating global regimes for the management of critical new industries and in dealings with their constituent enterprizes.

One critical point needs to be made at this stage of the discussion of regionalisation and its economic and technological driving forces. Many of the propositions that relate developments in the world economy, or its technological base, to increasing regionalisation can apply with equal force to arguments favouring further global, rather than regional, integration. Thus, effective control of regulation of the global economy might best be pitched at the global level. Enterprizes faced with the emergence of intensifying large-scale competition might be better advised to seek salvation through a global scale of response rather than confine their efforts to the regional level.

Regionalisation within the contemporary international system thus raises fundamental questions about the nature and effect of a range of central developments. Many of these developments appear to confront the traditional, established states with serious challenges. The response that such states should make, or are likely to make, is, however, by no means an easy question. Ultimately, the most appropriate level of response to a range of central contemporary developments in the international system will turn upon the likely effectiveness of each possible level of operation: sub-state, state, region, trans-regional alliance or global.

Regionalisation – problems and solutions

While the increasing regionalisation of the world appears to offer answers to a number of pressing problems, the process also carries its own problems and pitfalls, some of which may slow, or ultimately prevent, the emergence of a fully regionalised world.

The problems with macro-regionalisation

The further fragmentation of the world is the first, and most obvious, danger of regionalisation. The creation of any region within the world system may require many of the same processes that marked the formation of many modern nation states. A sense of cohesion and common identity has often been promoted by a sense of what is shared amongst the members of any community and what differentiates them from 'outsiders'. Indeed, many contemporary states have consolidated themselves through competition, and often outright conflict, with other societies. Moreover, if intensifying competition within the world political economy does prove to be the strongest stimulus to regionalisation in the future, it is only too likely to carry divisive implications.

Fragmentation within the world system might have a political and/or an economic complexion. Indeed, the pattern of fragmentation might differ, initially at least, in the political and economic domains. The patterns and speed of pressures for political regionalisation might vary markedly from those stimulating economic regionalisation. Thus, an outbreak of political instability and possible military conflict in a number of areas of the world might prompt rapid moves towards the creation of more effective regional security systems. The further intensification of competition within the international economy, or the emergence of serious economic disturbances, might encourage the deepening of a number of the current experiments with regional economic integration. While such developments in the political and economic domains are likely to impact upon one another ultimately, their developments might follow divergent paths in the shorter term.

Views about the political and economic impact of greater self-regarding regionalisation vary considerably. Political regionalisation offers a promising way forward for those who believe that the majority of established states now lack the resources to sustain credible security policies and provisions but who doubt the viability of world-wide security structures, such as those that have been attempted by the League of Nations and the United Nations in the past. By placing security arrangements on a more viable and realistic plane, advocates of regional security structures believe that political regionalisation will actually enhance security and stability for regional populations and the wider world 'community'.

Other anlaysts believe that political regionalisation would prove to be unavoidably divisive. New regional systems with defence and security structures would merely replicate the ill-effects of armed states at a higher level of organisation, thereby posing an enhanced, potential threat to other states and embryonic regions within the international system. Such perceived threats would merely stimulate responses in kind, with other states forming armed regions to confront those that had already emerged. The new regional powers would be so visible as to rule out any possibilities that tension could be reduced by mere inattention and would be so strong and influential as to further undermine the authority and capacities of agencies like the United Nations.[31]

The consequences of economic regionalisation are equally controversial. Many early advocates of the economic integration of Western Europe argued that such a process would contribute positively to the greater liberalisation and integration of the world economy. The promotion of free trade within the European Economic Community would, it was argued, sharpen the competitive capabilities of Europe's industries and create a more welcoming atmosphere towards wider economic liberalisation. Moreover, the combined weight of the European Economic Community would allow the exercise of considerable influence in favour of greater world-wide free trade within such negotiating fora as the General Agreement on Tariffs and Trade.

Not everyone has, however, been convinced that regional integration would lead to freer trade in the wider international economy. The view that regional economic integration was primarily a response to intensifying international economic competition fitted well with a neo-mercantilist vision of a future of deepening inter-regional economic conflicts of interest, in which a range of neo-mercantilist practices might become the norm to the detriment of genuine world-wide free trade. Indeed, success in freeing trade within a relatively cohesive region, with developing political and social institutions, might itself suggest some of the substantial obstacles of securing comparable liberalisation of the economic relations amongst regions that lacked, and that were unlikely to develop, any common political and social institutions. The term 'Fortress Europe' sums up many of the currents of potential divisiveness within a regionalised world.

The paths of political and economic regionalisation ultimately intersect, however, for both the optimists and the pessimists. For the optimists, successful political regionalisation will complement advancing economic regionalisation to demonstrate to peoples the benefits of integration and the advantages to be gained from moving on from the regional to the global level. To pessimists, in contrast, the successful political regionalisation will pit regions against regions in the security and defence realms, generating and intensifying inter-regional suspicions, hostilities and, ultimately, conflicts. Economic regionalisation will equally reflect and reinforce intensifying competition within the world political economy and give birth to self-regarding and mutually hostile economic blocks, which will undermine the cohesiveness of the world economy and lead, ultimately, to its disintegration into increasingly exclusive regional realms of economic activity.

INTERNAL COMPLICATIONS

Moves towards greater regional integration also have contradictory possibilities for harmony and cohesion within potential regions. The advocacy of regional structures, and supporting popular identities, poses a challenge to traditional state-level structures and identities which may be resisted by parts, sometimes substantial parts, of the populations so affected. There are two strands to such resistance to the regionalisation of structures and identities. Some may attach considerable intrinsic value to more 'traditional' identities, with their evocation of the past achievements of the relevant societies. Others, however, may be more anxious about abandoning structures and identities, which, for all their other possible shortcomings, have provided a substantial measure of support and security for their peoples, and gambling general well-being upon largely untried regional institutions.

A further, and no less serious, danger faced by the pursuit of regionalisation is that the processes of integration, and their short-term effects, may be such as to engender popular disenchantment with the regional experiment. Such problems can arise in the political and economic realms. The history of the European Community (latterly European Union) is replete with examples of policies promulgated at Community (Union) level which appear to challenge 'traditional' policies and preferences of one or other member societies, with proposed new rules about acceptable levels of alcohol for drivers of motor vehicles a recent, and controversial, example. Indeed, controversy about the acceptability of Community (Union) level policy-making at the time of the negotiation of the Maastricht Treaty on the further development of the Community led to the formulation of the principle of subsidiarity: the principle that policies should be determined at the political level that was most appropriate for any policy-issue and, therefore, be formulated at Community (Union) level only when strictly necessary.

In the economic realm, the pursuit of Economic and Monetary Union (EMU – the common currency) with the European Community exemplifies the range of difficulties that can be created by the promotion of regional economic integration. Initial resistance to the EMU project reflected popular concerns about the loss of a central symbol of 'national' sovereignty and more technical, but ultimately more important, anxieties about the economic dangers of forcing structurally dissimilar economies together into one common currency area, with (necessarily) broadly similar macro-economic policies. Popular opposition to EMU in a number of the referenda to ratify the Maastricht Treaty in a number of member countries was, indeed, such as to throw doubt upon the progress of the Treaty for a while.

The eventual implementation of EMU may further strain European integration, rather than contribute to its consolidation. The further integration of the economies of the participating societies will enhance competitive pressures and thus increase the pressures upon less-competitive producers and less vigorous regions. The collapse of firms and the attendant losses of jobs resulting from the further opening of markets may well stimulate popular resentment within those areas that are initial net losers from the integration experiment.

Moreover, uneven patterns of advantage and disadvantage from the advent of a more integrated European economy and market may be reinforced by the differential impact of changes in the world economy upon structurally dissimilar member economies. Thus, a sudden increase in world oil prices would have a far greater impact upon an economy that was heavily dependent upon imported oil for its energy supplies than upon an economy that employed coal or nuclear power as its major source of energy for industry. Again, an economy that was heavily committed to agricultural exports would be adversely affected by a sudden fall in world prices for agricultural products, while those member societies that were substantial importers of agricultural products might find themselves to be actual beneficiaries of such changes.

It is also possible that, in the absence of a sufficiently well-developed sense of community the region, and its institutions, will be blamed for developments for which it has no direct responsibility. A wave of increased unemployment resulting from the application of new, labour-saving technologies might thus be a function of the combined effects of the accelerating rate of technological innovation and intensifying competitive pressures within the wider world economy. The experience of worsened employment prospects of the populations of some of the regional member societies might, nevertheless, be blamed upon the regional institutions and their policies.

Many of the adverse consequences of combining structurally dissimilar economies within one larger, monetarily integrated, economy have been ameliorated traditionally by compensatory and redistributional policies orchestrated by central governments. For such policies to be adopted and implemented effectively, central governments need to be able to generate popular support throughout the polities that they serve and, most particularly, secure the assent of those who will have to shoulder the greatest part of the financial costs of the compensatory and redistributional policies. Recent evidence within a number of the world's richer countries has indicated the difficulty of sustaining such assent even when the recipients are clearly members of the same, relatively well-established, society. The problems of securing such assent are worsened substantially, however, when those who will be called upon to fund compensatory policies do not, or do not yet, fully recognise themselves to be members of the same society as those who will be beneficiaries. The resentments that were directed by West Germans towards the costs of the economic integration of the former East Germany, and compensating the many East Germans for their attendant short-term losses, demonstrates the problems even amongst a population that was disposed to see East Germans no part of the same 'national grouping' and re-emergent society.[32]

The persistence and growth of suspicions of the North American Free Trade Area (NAFTA), particularly across the US/Mexican border, also illustrates the difficulties that can be generated by moves towards regional economic integration of a more modest character than that intended within the European Union. NAFTA illustrates the way in which any process of regional integration that goes beyond mere rhetoric, will have identifiable effects upon the viability of economic enterprizes, employment prospects and the well-being of various socio-economic groups in the societies involved. The effects will be complex, and their final balance of advantages and disadvantages may be even in some cases. People affected adversely by integration may not, however, see, or be impressed by, the benefits secured by others. Tensions are highly likely to be generated by experiments with regional economic integration. The effects of such tensions will, however, be a function of the size of the populations adversely affected, their physical locations and their capacities for political influence. Small groups of sufferers widely distributed throughout society may be readily containable. Geographically concentrated pockets of the disadvantaged and dispossesed may create far greater local problems, but it might be possible to limit the geographical spread of discontent and adverse reaction. Where, however, a significant proportion of the population nationwide is affected, or acute problems develop within geographically sensitive areas, then the adverse consequences of regional economic integration might impose unacceptable political and economic costs upon the wider society and, in the extreme, prompt the repudiation of pro-integration policies and even the reversal of integration itself.

The problems with meso-regionalisation and micro-regionalisation

The attractions of both meso-regionalisation and micro-regionalisation rest upon their reflection of 'natural', indeed more 'natural', patterns of economic activity and/or communal identification than established states. Indeed, supporters of both meso-regions and micro-regions advocate them as inevitable complements to macro-regionalisation, by corresponding to those areas of synergistic economic vitality that have actually grown up within wider macro-regions, or by allowing macro-regions to be based upon more substantial and enduring patterns of cultural commonality and popular identity than those that compose of states. Meso-regionalism reflects a more functionalist approach to the patterning of the political economy, with its stress upon the force of economic developments; micro-regionalism rests more clearly upon a social constructionist basis with its emphasis upon the cultural and ideational foundations of social groups and their political and economic life.[33]

Both meso-regionalism and micro-regionalism may, however, pose threats to the stability of macro-regions and established states alike. The crystallisation of viable macro-regions may actually be obstructed if meso-regions emerge and form into cohesive economic areas of considerable strength and influence within both the putative macro-region and the wider world economy. Such a meso-region, founded as it may well be upon competitive industries and innovative technologies, may prefer to make its way in the competitive world economy unencumbered by the poorer and economically weaker regions of a heterogeneous macro-region. Competitiveness and prosperity within the meso-region may be enhanced by the speed and flexibility of policy response, and lack of costly appendages that freedom from the wider region might bring.

The emergence of strong meso-regions will also cut across established state frontiers, weakening the authority and possibly the competence of state governments. Such new cross-border associations may be welcome to opponents of the traditional state. However, if such new associations undermine the political institutions of established states they may create a political void that can be filled only by the creation of new arrangements for the governance of meso-regions and the management of their relations with other parts of the world.

Micro-regions might also undermine effective macro-regionalisation as local particularisms come into conflict with the region-wide policies and perspectives of the political institutions of the macro-region. Indeed, the emergence of cohesive micro-regions could well intensify divisive responses to any difficulties encountered by the macro-region as it pursues greater integration. Uneven experiences of developments like the adoption of a common currency, or some external economic 'shock', will fuel local resentments, ambitions and responses and pitch sentiments against the macro-region and its institutions of government.

Established states are equally to be weakened by the rise of micro-regionalism, if it moves beyond mere local government on a regional scale. More ambitious forms of micro-regionalisation are unlikely to enjoy the potential strengths and capabilities of prosperous meso-regions. Their capabilities are thus likely to be substantially inferior to those of the established states that they replace. If the emergence of micro-regions does not itself compromise the crystallisation of effective macro-regions, then all might be well. However, if active micro-regionalism undermines effective macro-regions, then a patch-work of mini-states might emerge, which, like many of Europe's current mini-states, would be incapable of effective self-defence in military terms, lack sufficient weight to bargain effectively with large Transnational Corporations and other transnationally mobile economic interests and be denied significant influence in any but moral terms upon the wider world stage.

The dangers of meso-regionalism and micro-regionalism are not confined to their effects upon intended macro-regions or established states, however. They also carry dangers for one another. Both meso-regions and micro-regions gain the logic of their existence from something distinctive that they, or their members, possess: particularly beneficial patterns of mutual economic activity; or common cultural heritage. Such characteristics have exclusive as well as inclusive implications. Others would be defined as those who lack such characteristics and who therefore warrant different treatment. The path to mutually exclusive policies and patterns of behaviour is thus evident within the foundational conditions of meso-regionalism and micro-regionalism and, with the weakening of stabilising state structures and the possible failure of new macro-region polities, could well lead to mutual hostility, and ultimately conflict.

Notes

1 For discussions of the possible connections between globalisation and regionalisation see: R.J. Barry Jones, *Globalisation and Interdependence in the International Political Economy: Rhetoric and Reality* (London: Pinter, 1995), esp. pp. 141–53; and AndreWyatt-Walter, 'Regionalism, globalisation, and world economic order', in L. Fawcett and A. Hurrell (eds), *Regionalism in World Politics: Regional Organisation and International Order* (Oxford: Oxford University Press, 1995), pp. 74–121.

2 Corresponding, in a general way, to Kenichi Ohmae's notion of 'regional economies', Kenichi Ohmae, *The End of the Nation State: The Rise of Regional Economies* (London: Harper Collins; Free Press in the USA, 1995).

3 On the European experience see: William Wallace, 'Regionalism in Europe: model or exception?', in Fawcett and Hurrell, *Regionalism in World Politics*, pp. 201–27; and Stephen George, 'The European Union, 1992 and the fear of

"Fortress Europe"', in Gamble and Payne, *Regionalism and World Order* (Harmondsworth: Macmillan, 1996), pp. 21–54.

4 For a succinct account of the origins of post-war European integration see: John Pinder, *European Community: The Building of a Union* (Oxford: Oxford University Press, 1991), chapter 1.

5 The reports in *The Economist*: 'If', 22 August 1992, p. 19; 'Awaiting the German Ja', 22 May 1993, pp. 41–2; and 'Last harrumph for Maastricht', 16 October 1993, p. 46.

6 *The Economist*: 'Those Vikings are at it again', 7 November 1992, p. 47.

7 See, for example, the reports in *The Economist*: 'The end of never-never land', 13 February 1993, pp. 17–18; 'Which way to EMU?', 13 February 1993, pp. 77–8; 'A funny new EMU', 4 March 1995, pp. 35–6; 'A dying deadling?', 20 January 1996, pp. 47–8; 'The EMU backsliders', 23 March 1996, p. 44; 'EMU without tear-gas?', 1 June 1996, pp. 41–4; and 'What's the German for fudge?', 8 June 1996, pp. 51–2.

8 See the report in *The Economist*: 'E pluribus unum', 8 January 1994, pp. 35–6.

9 *Handbook of International Trade and Development Statistics, 1991* (New York: UNCTAD, 1992), table 3.4, pp. 112–25.

10 *The Economist, World in Figures 1997* (London: Economist, 1996).

11 Jones, *Globalisation and Interdepence*, table 6.5, p. 116.

12 For a survey of regionalisation in the Americas see: Andrew Hurrell, 'Regionalism in the Americas', in Fawcett and Hurrell (eds), *Regionalism in World Politics*, pp. 250–82; on the role of the USA see: Anthony Payne, 'The United States and its enterprise for the Americas', in Gamble and Payne (eds), *Regionalism and World Order*, pp. 93–129; and on Latin America specifically see: Jean Grugel, 'Latin America and the remaking of the Americas', in Gamble and Payne (eds), *Regionalism and World Order*, pp. 131–67; and Diana Tussie, 'In the whirlwind of globalisation and multilateralism: the case of emerging regionalism in Latin America', in W.D. Coleman and G.R.D. Underhill (eds), *Regionalism and Global Economic Integration* (London: Routledge, 1998), pp. 81–96.

13 *The Economist*, 'World in Figures' *1997*.

14 Jones, *Globalisation and Interdependence*, table 6.28, p. 154.

15 UNCTAD, *Handbook of International Trade and Development Statistics, 1991* (New York: UNCTAD, 1992), annex table A.1, pp. A4–A5.

16 For general surveys see: Rosemary Foot, 'Pacific Asia: The development of regional dialogue', in Fawcett and Hurrell, *Regionalism in World Politics*, pp. 228–49.

17 See, for example, table 6.27 in Jones, *Globalisation and Interdpendence*, p. 152.

18 UNCTAD, *Handbook of International Trade and Development Statistics, 1991* (New York: UNCTAD, 1992), table 3.4, pp. 112–25.

19 *The Economist*, report: 'Pointless?', 27 July 1996, pp. 59–60.

20 *The Economist*, report: 'Will East Asia keep its balance?', 26 July 1997, pp. 65–6.

21 For a general survey see: Charles Tripp, 'Regional organisations in the Arab Middle East', in Fawcett and Hurrell, *Regionalism in World Politics*, pp. 283–308.

22 UNCTAD, *Handbook of International Trade and Developments Statistics*, 1991, table 3.4, pp. 112–25.

23 See: table 2, Andrew Wyatt-Walter, 'Regionalism and world order', pp. 102–3.

24 See: Ian Kearns, 'Eastern Europe in transition into the New Europe', in Gamble and Payne (eds), *Regionalism and World Order*, pp. 55–91.

25 Ohmae, *The End of the Nation State*, esp. chapter 7.
26 Although the British Trades Union Congress – the confederal organisation of its trades unions had, by the late 1990s adopted a pro-integration stance and, in particular, an enthusiastic attitude towards British membership of Euope's monetary union. The genellay hostile attitude of organised labour within the United States of America towards the Northa American Free Trade Area stands in marked contrast with this position.
27 For a wide-randing review of functionalist theory and practice see: A.J.R. Groom and P. Taylor (eds), *Functionalism: Theory and Practice in International Relations* (London: University of London Press, 1975).
28 For discussions of a number of aspects of neo-functionalism see: R.O. Keohane and S. Hoffman (eds), *The New Europe Community: Decisionmaking and Institutional Change* (Boulder, CO: Westview, 1991).
29 On which see: Pinder, *European Community*, chapter 1.
30 See *The Economist* report: 'Peace in our time', 26 July 1997, pp. 79–81.
31 For a discussion of the prospects for a regionalised world see: Charles A. Kupchan, 'After Pax American: benign power, regional integration and the sources of a stable multipolarity', in B. Hansen and B. Heurlin, *The New World Order: Contrasing Theories* (Houndmills: Macmillan, 2000), pp. 134–66.
32 On the problems of economic and, in particular, monetary integration, see: Barry Eichengreen, *European Monetary Unification: Theory, Practice, and Analysis* (Cambridge, MA: The MIT Press, 1997).
33 For the intellectual foundations of which see: Peter L. Berger and Thomas Luckmann, *The Social Construction of Reality: A Treatise in the Sociology of Knowledge* (Harmondsworth: Penguin Book, 1967); and John R. Searle, *The Construction of Social Reality* (Harmondsworth: Allen Lane, Penguin Press, 1995).

Further reading

Fawcett, L. and Hurrell, A. (eds), *Regionalism in World Politics: Regional Organisation and International Order* (Oxford: Oxford University Press, 1995). A valuable collection of discussion of contemporary regionalisation.

Gamble, A. and Payne, A. (eds), *Regionalism and World Order* (London: Macmillan, 1996). A further collection of value on contemporary regionalisation.

Ohmae, Kenichi, *The End of the Nation State: The Rise of Regional Economies* (London: Harper Collins, 1995). An interesting argument on the end of the nation-state and its replacement by regional economies.

Scolopino, Robert, 'The United States and Asia: future prospects', *Foreign Affairs*, 70, 5. (Winter, 1991–2): 19–40.

7 Fragmentation in world affairs

Patterns

The ending of the Cold War, the re-emergence of many religious and tribal divisions and the progress of globalisation have encouraged a widespread belief that the world is now so complex, with so many diverse patterns of development, that traditional perspectives upon world affairs have become obsolete and many simple expectations of future developments unwarranted. A diversity of terms has been employed to denote this complex and uncertain world, but the notion of fragmentation captures most of the important points: fragmentation of the power and position of states; fragmentation of any neat, linear paths of future development; and, hence, the fragmentation of intellectual approaches to world affairs.[1]

Fragmentation can be detected in a wide range of contemporary conditions and intellectual responses. Pessimistic observers identify a clear, and possibly accelerating, pattern of social fragmentation within the world's advanced industrial societies. Data on delinquency, crime, welfare dependency, and even the rise of support for regional autonomy, are often quoted in support of the view that the domestic solidarity that many Western societies enjoyed in the past, and particularly during and immediately after the Second World War, is now a thing of the past. Problems of such data, and the tendency to idealise the past notwithstanding, the weakening of domestic bonds may be associated with many the forces that have now been unleashed within the world's political, economic and 'cultural' system, with particular concern focusing upon the possible emergence of a persistent 'underclass' of a sizeable group of unemployed (and unemployable) people living more-or-less permanently on the margins of modern consumer societies.

The earlier discussion of globalisation summarised many of the arguments about the manner in which some of the features of contemporary globalisation have posed a challenge to the 'traditional' capabilities of the state in the areas of economic and industrial management. These features, and any associated reduction of state strength, may be further evidence of contemporary fragmentation. If the state's abilities to manage important areas of policy and, hence, satisfy the expectations of its citizens, is under threat, then political fragmentation may be reinforced and accelerated. Certainly, the disaffection of the populations of economically disadvantaged regions within the advanced industrial world and within many LDCs attests to such a fragmentary effect, as does the revival of calls for regional autonomy within wider regions that feel let down by central state authorities or believe that a globalising and/or regionalising world offers them new opportunities that can best be exploited through bypassing established states.

It is also possible to detect a crisis of international governance; governance being defined generally as the authoritative provision of desired and/or necessary collective goods for any collectivity, public or private.[2] Established international organisations have been, overwhelmingly, inter-state (or inter-governmental) organisations, dependent for their resources, and often for their capacities for practical action, upon traditional states. Some of the new weaknesses of the state in a globalising world can be overcome, partially, by the existence and operation of international organisations. Ultimately, however, any substantial weakening of states will weaken the international organisations that they sustain, unless these organisations can achieve a remarkable transformation into agencies of genuinely global governance and, possibly, some new global democracy.[3] The emergence of genuinely global forms of governance remains some way off and will continue to confront massive obstacles for the foreseeable future. The weakening of states would thus be likely to weaken international organisations and their limited role in international governance, leaving the field open to private, self-interested forms of international management (by such agencies as multinational corporations, producer cartels, private financial agencies), the limited activities of public interest non-governmental organisations (like Green Peace) or to an intensified form of international and transnational anarchy.[4]

The possible weakening of effective international governance by the community of states and their representatives both reflects and is a partial cause of the political and social fragmentation that has characterised the last decade of the twentieth century and the first years of the twenty-first. The collapse of the former Yugoslavia into myriad warring ethnic and religious factions and mini-states; inter-communal violence across much of the former Soviet Union; the disintegration of political power, social cohesion and economic functioning in many African states; and, before the new century was really underway, the eruption of renewed violence between Israel and its Palestinian neighbours, all attest to the turbulence and fragmentation of the immediate post-Cold War era. The economic and financial crisis of East and South East Asia in 1997 and 1998 also demonstrated the chaotic and destructive potential lurking at the heart of an increasingly integrated global financial system.

The intellectual response to contemporary developments in world affairs is also fragmentary. The variety of analytical perspectives upon international affairs has expanded noticeably, with the disappearance of the disciplines (and dangers) of the Cold War. At the extreme, the popularity of post-modernism as an intellectual disposition, provides a clear, if extreme, signal a form of fragmentation within the intellectual approach to world affairs[5] as well as within its subject matter.

There are many indicators of the practical and intellectual fragmentation at the end of the twentieth century. Traditional diplomacy, in which trained civil servants negotiate with each other, has become less important because the communications and transportation revolutions have allowed top political officials to do more of that work directly. Those same revolutions have also made it easier for people outside the foreign policy elite to become involved in, admittedly, more informal diplomatic activity.

Track-two and citizen diplomacy have been the most productive so far.[6] As usually defined, track-two initiatives involve informal and at most semi-official contacts between groups from opposing states. Often, the representatives are academics who meet in the guise of a scholarly conference. Citizen diplomacy is more open and, as the name suggests, involves average citizens, not diplomats or academic experts. Typically, it includes grass roots efforts to bring people from the conflicting states into contact with each other to break down the stereotypes and other barriers that hinder cooperation and, in time, put pressure on their leaders to reach some sort of formal, negotiated settlement to their dispute.

Citizen diplomacy burst on to the scene during the renewal of Cold War tensions in the 1980s. Recall that relations between the superpowers deteriorated in the late 1970s and led to the massive arms build-up by the Reagan administration and a corresponding hard line taken by the ageing leadership in the Kremlin.

The tensions produced a number of reactions from people in both countries who were worried about the heightened possibility of nuclear war. There were protest movements, for example, in all the Western European countries where the new US Cruise and Pershing II missiles would be deployed.

For our purposes, it also produced the first significant citizen diplomacy initiative. Throughout the United States and, to a lesser degree, the Soviet Union, efforts were made to bring people from various walks of life together. The International Physicians for the Prevention of Nuclear War won the Nobel Peace Prize for their efforts to mobilise doctors. Similar initiatives developed in most other professions. These extended beyond the groups one often associated with the peace movement (e.g. teachers) to include Business Executives for Nuclear Sanity and Rotarians for Peace. Sometimes, citizen diplomacy involved specific projects. For example, the California-based Beyond War Foundation brought together a team of Soviet and American scholars to write the first joint book on a political theme, which was published to a considerable fanfare in both countries.

Citizen diplomacy is now common practice whenever political circumstances permit it. The National Business Initiative helped bring Afrikaners and Blacks together in South Africa in the tumultuous days between the release of Nelson Mandela in 1991 and the first free election four years later. Similarly, in 1998, Benetton and Newsweek published a magazine-length feature on efforts being made to bring Palestinians and Israelis together (all were wearing Benetton clothes of course). Finally, the Good Friday agreement in Northern Ireland has seen a redoubling of efforts to reduce tensions by increasing contacts between Catholics and Protestants.

No one knows how important citizen diplomacy is or can be. It rarely receives much attention from the press or academic researchers. It does seem clear that it rarely has an immediate impact on formal negotiations carried out by diplomats and politicians. However, if the research on the changing mood of the US electorate during the 1980s is at all accurate, it can have a significant impact on public opinion and, hence, the overall strategies pursued by policy makers. The efforts of Beyond War, again, are instructive. From 1983 through 1988, Beyond War conducted three weekly sessions that constituted an 'orientation to a world beyond war' in communities scattered around fourteen American states. In all, perhaps 500,000 people attended those seminars, many of whom were what marketing researchers call 'opinion leaders' and 'innovators' in their communities. While no more than 5 per cent of those people went on to become Beyond War activists, the available anecdotal evidence suggests that a much higher proportion started applying Beyond War's ideas about conflict resolution in general to their daily lives and campaigning for improved US–Soviet relations in the political realm.

Track-two diplomacy came of age in the 1990s. Again, it is hard to tell just how important contacts between academics and others who have some, but usually, informal contacts with decision makers can be. However, unlike citizens' initiatives, we can identify examples in which track-two diplomacy led to major, official breakthroughs.

There is no better example than that of the Oslo agreement reached between Israel and the PLO in 1993. As events since then have demonstrated, Oslo did not settle the Arab–Israeli dispute. However, it did propel relations between Palestinians and Jews toward a more normal footing than anything attempted before or after.

Fragmentation – contemporary forms

- ***Political***
  States are losing economic control, regulative capacity and ability to secure the well-being of their citizens – many states are also being riven by revived religious and ethnic disputes
- ***Economic***
  The world is actually fragmenting into separate and mutually antagonistic societies, groups and individuals, under the pressures of globalisation
- ***Social***
  Societies are loosing cohesiveness as globalisation brings both increased pressure and new opportunities for consumption and transnational communication
- ***Intellectual***
  The unifying certainties of the past are dissolving with the disappearance of the Cold War into history, the global transmission of pluralistic images and intellectual references, and the (temporary) absence of any major political and military threats to the populations of most of the advanced industrial countries

Sources

Many of the innovations, conditions and processes that are associated with globalisation also lie at the heart of possible fragmentation. Fragmentation is largely the result of social and global forces that, as has been suggested, have rendered some states so powerless that they have all but ceased to exist, and many others seriously circumscribed in what they can hope to do, particularly if seeking to act alone.

Care, however, is necessary if a discriminating view is to be developed of the current level, and future prospects, of fragmentation upon the world stage. A critical review of the supposed sources of contemporary fragmentation, can reveal some of the uncertainties about contemporary developments, their implications and future prospects.

The new technologies of information gathering, processing and transmission have been widely identified as a major source of many recent developments upon the world stage.[7] Such technologies underpin the recent surge towards greater globalisation, particularly in the areas of global financial integration and increased transnational organisation of industrial production. Increased transnational integration of industrial activity, and the greater scale of operation of the leading industrial conglomerates, have also encouraged what some see as the emergence of a new global consumer culture.

The new technologies of communication have also facilitated a huge increase in the capacity for direct transnational communication amongst people. Such contacts may, again, complement any tendencies towards the emergence of a global culture and a global society.[8]

At one level, these forms of intensified global integration look like the opposite of fragmentation. However, as the Asian economic and financial crisis of 1997 and 1998 demonstrated, such high levels of financial and industrial integration can expose societies, their governments and peoples, to greater strains and pressures and lead, all too easily, to massive economic, social and political dislocation.[9]

The increased scale of transnational industrial production also carries fragmentary threats within its integrative persona. At one level, those who work in a transnationally integrated production process are intimately bound together. Frequently, however, the production process is so organised as to leave most, if not all, of its employees vulnerable to divide and rule strategies. Those who seek improved conditions of work may be told that their plant might be closed down and the work transferred to facilities in another country, with more compliant workers. Output levels achieved in one plant can be used as a benchmark to insist on higher levels of output or productivity elsewhere. Overall, an atmosphere of acute insecurity may be fostered within the workforce by the transnational mode of activity of employing firms and the possibilities of rapid re-sourcing of components that this may bring.

The possibilities of increased inter-personal communication via the internet also has fragmentary implications, as internet contacts facilitate the emergence of highly specialised, often deviant and sometimes politically extreme, interest groups. Improved international communications have combined with global financial integration to facilitate increased transnational criminal association and activity and, in particular, the deployment of illicit financial resources. Such developments may be integrative for the groups involved, but may have highly fragmentary implications for the wider society.

Not all of the sources of the current appearance of fragmentary tendencies within world affairs lie within developments in the world's economy, however. Political and intellectual conditions are also an important source of fragmentary sentiments.

The ending of the Cold War freed the world of one of its most pressing problems and sources of potential danger, but it also removed a major source of stability in the conduct of international relations and a linchpin of intellectual certainty. The diverse tendencies and developments that have been witnessed during the relatively brief post-Cold War era underpin a general sense that, far from witnessing the birth of a 'new world order', the world may have been plunged into a new era of endemic disorder and fragmentation.[10] Many of the post-Cold War developments were, however, encouraged if not actually caused by the removal of the disciplining influence of the Cold War. Feelings of general disorder may, moreover, owe much to the current (but possibly temporary) absence of any pivotal line of confrontation within world affairs and/or pressing threat to the leading powers.

Notions of general fragmentation are also notoriously cyclical in their occurrence. Periods of pessimism about the human condition in general, or the state of specific societies, are common and may be attributable to specific conditions: periods of relatively rapid change in common technologies, political institutions or patterns of social behaviour. Paradoxically they may be encouraged by the absence of serious external threats to the societies within which such pessimistic currents arise. Moreover, a general sense of fragmentation may be more common in societies that are relatively prosperous and economically successful, than in those experiencing serious economic difficulties, in which attention tends to focus upon a narrower, more tangible set of conditions and problems.

Most specifically, a general sense of fragmentation in social, political and world affairs may, itself, be a function of prevailing patterns of political performance. Certainly the neo-liberal fashion[11] within the politics of a number of influential industrial countries in the 1980s and early 1990s contributed, substantially, to the advance of a number of the conditions and processes conventionally associated with globalisation. Moreover, a general reaction against the role of the state in a number of Western societies may have contributed to a weakening of public authority and, hence, some of the apparent symptoms of fragmentation within societies. Economic and technological developments do not, in short, take place in a vacuum: prevailing political principles and practices are a large part of the environment that shapes and facilitates the practical application of technology and the course of economic developments.

Despite the diversity of recent developments, and the range of interpretations to which they give rise, there are clear signs of potential fragmentation upon the world scene. Any such fragmentation is neither simple, as has been seen, nor irreversible. It is to the problems created by fragmentation, and to the possible reactions and solutions that might result, that the discussion therefore has to turn.

Problems and solutions

If fragmentation within international relations and the domestic circumstances of established states is a growing trend, then the world is clearly faced with a number of pressing problems and/or exciting possibilities. Anarchists and extreme libertarians may welcome the collapse of the state and the possible emergence of new web-like arrangements for the collective management of human affairs, locally, regionally and globally.[12] There, are, however, many substantial obstacles to the emergence of such a post-state utopia, not least those of effective coordination, resolution of differences of interest and opinion and, ultimately, the control of violent tendencies.

The core problem is that any further diminution of the role and capacity of the state will have two serious consequences: internationally, it will weaken the one institution upon which most contemporary institutions for international management are ultimately based; domestically it will undermine the position of the ultimate guarantor of personal protection for the greater part of the population and general peace and harmony. More specifically, the modern state, for all its weaknesses and excesses, has emerged as the major provider of a range of critical public goods for their citizens and the forum within which the most central decisions are reached about what conditions should be considered to be legitimate public goods and, when so defined, how they should best be provided.

Public goods, in this sense, are those collective goods – conditions and/or services that once provided have to be available to all the members of a community, cannot be provided on a piece-meal basis, and which may require costly contributions from most, if not all, the members of that community for their provision.[13] Public goods, then, are those collective goods that can only be provided through public agencies, like the state, or are thought to be most effectively provided by such agencies. The purest forms of public goods, such as those of national security, are not only non-excludable in character (the protection afforded cannot readily be removed from anyone who remains a member of the community) but may well be such that their enjoyment by one individual in no way reduces the level of enjoyment available to all others (jointedness).

There is nothing in principle that is unique about the modern state in its ability to ensure the provision of valued public goods, it is merely that states have, for a range of historical reasons, occupied the centre of stage in this respect during the twentieth century and beyond. The problem, then, is that the 'success' of the state has dislodged and often eliminated alternative structures for the provision of valued public goods (transnational religious movements, for instance).[14] With the collapse of international ideologies like Marxism–Leninism, there are, indeed, even fewer organising principles for non-state provision of public goods at the end of the twentieth century than there were in earlier decades.

Many, but not all states, have, however, developed at a scale and a size that does enable them to act effectively on a range of issues that are, or may be, of concern to their citizens. This is particularly true of their embrace of areas and regions with sufficient differences of geographical location or socio-economic circumstances to permit support to be provided to areas that encounter particular problems. The ability of the government of the United States of America to define a number of flooded areas of the country's eastern seaboard as 'disaster areas' and then provide effective assistance from its accumulated resources and/or resources drawn currently from other areas of the country, exemplifies the cross-support that modern states of sufficient size and effectiveness can provide to the regionally or circumstantially disadvantaged.

Not everyone bemoans the weakening of the state, however. Some identify the modern state with the sharp distinctions that have often been drawn between the peoples of different societies and, hence, the seeds of virulent nationalisms and large scale international conflict. For such critical observers of the state, therefore, its weakening holds the promise of reduced inter-societal antagonisms and less frequent international conflicts.[15]

Such idealistic expectations have, however, been dulled a little by the horrifying consequences of state collapse in a number of LCDs and, in particular, areas of the former Soviet Union. However, whether such cataclysms are best to be attributed to simple state collapse or, in contrast, to efforts to construct alternative states to those previously existing, remains a debatable question.

The problem, then, remains whether a world characterised by international and/or domestic fragmentation will retain, or be able to create new, public agencies capable of providing desirable, and even necessary, public goods for its citizens.[16] If vacuums develop in the area of international and/or domestic governance only four other possibilities remain: the crystallisation of a new pattern of what has come to be known as multi-level governance, in which different authorities at different levels of public life and of differeing form and composition undertake, in some kind of collaborative arrangement, those functions of public governance for which they are most suited; the emergence of wholly new structures for the provision of public goods that are not formal public authorities, like the state, but are formed from less formal networks of engaged people; the movement into the vacuum of public governance of essentially private interests and agencies, ranging from transnational corporations, through private interest groupings (like international sports' authorities), to transnational criminal associations, like international mafias; or a descent into anarchy, internationally and/or within established societies.

MULTI-LEVEL GOVERNANCE

The prospects for a new pattern of multi-level governance has begun to attract increasing attention. The hope is that the complex task of governance required by a world characterised by both globalisation and regionalisation can be undertaken by a layer-cake of authorities, each operating at the level for which it is best suited.[17] The model for such a new arrangement is often held to be that of the emerging pattern of governance within the European Union. The complexities of governance within the EU reflect the co-existence of the non-elected European Commission, the elected European Parliament and the state-nominated Council of Ministers, along with the continued existence and substantial authority of purely national political and governmental systems. The concept of subsidiarity expresses the philosophy of multi-level governance by authorising, in theory at least, the exercise of authority at the most appropriate level of political life.

The problems of multi-level governance in practice within the European Union, however, illustrate its possible difficulties as a model for the future management of the world's affairs. Tensions continue to exist between national political systems and European-level institutions and unresolved questions about which level of governance will prevail in the case of serious disputes over issues that are deemed to be of fundamental importance (echoing the uncertainties that affected the United States of America before the Civil War). Uncertainties about the complex pattern of governance, moreover, reflect the persistence of suspicions about the European project amongst the populations of many of the larger member states. The practical and emotional uncertainties created by multi-level governance thus cast serious doubts about its ultimate suitability as a model for future global governance.

NEW GOVERNANCE NETWORKS

As was seen in the earlier discussion of aspects of contemporary globalisation, some observers have high expectations of the potentialities of new inter-personal and inter-societal networks based upon the opportunities provided by the internet and by cheaper and more rapid forms of international transportation. Indeed, there is some evidence for the emergence of such networks, for example: the success of transnational non-governmental organisations, like Greenpeace, in mobilising pressure across national frontiers to secure changes of behaviour by oil companies like Shell and BP; and the achievements of the anti-globalisation coalition in generating widespread 'popular' opposition to further globalisation and, in particular, preparing a critical approach to future rounds of trade liberalisation negotiations under the auspices of the World Trade Organisation.

International travel has also expanded massively in recent decades. Air travel and high speed trains have substantially enhanced the ability of people to move considerable distances, speedily and at relatively low costs. The spectacular growth of the package-holiday industry has provided tangible evidence of this increase in mobility.

Neither the emergence of new transnational interest networks, nor the growth of international travel is without its difficulties, however, and neither carries an unambiguous message for the future of new forms of international and transnational public governance.[18]

There are two problems, in particular, with many of the new transnational interest networks.[19] First, although some of the more prominent can point to a record of general influence upon opinion in specific areas – like the environmental activists on the causes and dangers of global warming – such success is often uneven, as witnessed by the quite different levels of concern about the genetic modification of food in Europe and the United States of America – and its impact may often not be more than marginal or intermittent – as suggested by the relatively modest undertakings on carbon emissions agreed at the Rio Conference on the environment and UN declarations in late 1999 that even these targets were unlikely to be met.[20]

Second, and rather more seriously, is the very real danger that the proliferation of transnational interest networks will reinforce fragmentary tendencies, rather than prove to be their corrective. The problem is that many transnational networks are specialised in their areas of concern and highly particular in the views that they advance on issues of interest. Transnational networks of paedophiles or political extremists are merely the extreme case of such partiality and of the very real possibility that the proliferation of such networks will merely encourage the emergence of counter-networks. The overall effect of the development of many such transnational networks may, therefore, be the reinforcement of disparate, and often incompatible, views and their transmission on a wider, international scale.

The growth of international travel and other forms of contact may also prove to be less than favourable to greater international and transnational harmony and better public governance. Many who travel on package-holidays engage in relatively little real contact with the natives of the countries that they visit and what contact they have is usually highly constrained by the rituals of hotel life and other tourist services. Worse, short encounters with the peoples and cultures of other societies can all too easily generate misunderstandings and clashes, and lead to the reinforcement of prejudices and unfavourable stereotypes. Few, if any, credible transnational networks for global public governance can be attributed to the fruits of package-holidays to foreign lands.

PRIVATE GOVERNANCE OF THE PUBLIC SPHERE

Many of the visions of the future, contained in the bleaker of the Hollywood films, envisage the effective governance of the public sphere by self-interested private agencies, like massive corporations. Such visions provide a highly dramatised indication of many of the difficulties and dangers associated with such an alternative approach to public governance. The central problems are those of the partiality of the interests that direct the private agencies that seek to undertake public governance – particularly profit and relative short-sightedness – as evidenced by repeated failures of private regulators of the financial industries; the limited resources for enforcing rules and regulations – unless the private agencies have succeeded in taking over armies and police forces – as envisaged in some Hollywood films; and, most seriously, the related lack of general legitimacy of such private agencies – their lack of democratic credentials and inability to command acceptance for disagreeable decisions and policies by their parallel provision of public goods that populations value highly.[21]

The prospects for private agencies in public governance are thus limited and fraught with dangers. Short-term success would, therefore, be likely to be followed by spectacular failure and/or popular

Problems with private global governance

- Private and partial interests prevail over those of the public
- Lack of foresight: the record of private regulative bodies in anticipating and pre-empting major problems is poor – as demonstrated by the world's stock exchanges and major financial institutions
- Lack of resources: few, if any, private agencies can impose universal taxes, recruit extensive armed forces, or maintain effective police forces for whole communities
- Lack of legitimacy: lack of proper authority and/or democratic credentials

rejection and resistance. Both eventualities would return the realm of public governance to a quasi-anarchical condition that would leave desirable, and often necessary, public goods unsupplied or seriously under-supplied.

A NEW ANARCHY

The problems of the regulation of the public sphere in the absence of effective public authorities has concerned political theorists down the ages, and particularly since the emergence of modern anarchist theory after the French Revolution. Optimism about the capacities for societies to undertake self-regulation through informal patterns of association, or, where necessary, through institutions that rest firmly upon 'bottom-up' patterns of authority, has been at the heart of the theories of anarchists, mutualists, syndicalists, guild socialists, some Marxists and American libertarians. Such optimism parallels that of those observers of contemporary developments who place faith in the possibility that new, internet based networks will form a new basis for human social interaction and mutual governance.

The problems facing such associational forms have also been long debated by political theorists. The issue turns around beliefs about the ultimate nature of human beings and about the complex interaction between that human nature and the institutions and arrangements that humanity has constructed over the millennia for the conduct of their economic, social and political lives. The intellectual problem turns around the impossibility, thus far, of differentiating 'human nature' from the circumstances within which human beings operate, and have to operate, in the world, past and present. Whether these circumstances reflect universal and timeless qualities of human beings, or whether they constitute merely one of a wide range of conditions that might be, and might have been, constructed by humanity, remains an intensely debated issue.[22]

Doubts about the possibilities of associational forms of collective governance, that regularly involve people directly in political decision-making, rest upon empirical and precautionary grounds. First, it is argued that instances of purely associational patterns of governance are so rare, and usually confined to such unusual societies, as to raise doubts about their suitability for the complex and dynamic societies of the modern world. The second ground is precautionary, contending that attempts to construct new forms of human governance on the basis of mere theoretical presumptions about human characteristics and potentialities is an inherently risky, and possibly foolhardy, enterprise. Empirical and precautionary arguments come together in critical interpretations of those past revolutionary moments at which attempts have been made to refound societies upon principles of association and self-governance, but which have resulted in disorder, tyranny and, too frequently, dictatorship.

A REASSERTION OF THE STATE?

If transnational networks offer an uncertain and problematical basis for future global governance, private agencies remain inherently suspect, and associational approaches to social self-regulation highly contentious in their presumptions and prospects, then institutions which are like states may, for all their well-rehearsed shortcomings, remain the best chance for effective future global governance. 'Institutions like states', it must be stressed, because a future world state would have characteristics that were different in important respects from states located within a system of other states.

The need for state-like institutions turns around their ability, when functioning effectively, to provide a range of public goods. It is this plurality of provisions that encourages citizens to accept costly impositions in some areas (restraints on personal freedoms, the necessity to pay taxes, etc.) as part of the price that has to be paid to secure the overall package of desired public goods that the state is providing. Such acceptance is, ultimately, the basis of the popular legitimacy of the state.

Advantages of states and state-like institutions

- Extent and range of resources available for public purposes
- Ability to deal with a range of needs and wants simultaneously (and, hence, capacity to offer trade-offs of obligations in some areas against valued services in others)
- Legitimacy and (increasingly) democratic credentials
- Foresight and planning in the public interest

Many of the growing problems upon the global stage would best be managed by a global state. The control of the global financial system and transnational corporations and the regulation of the world's natural environment would clearly be easier for a genuine world-wide authority that possessed the capacity to enforce its rules and regulations in every corner of the globe.

The prospects of a world state remain poor, however. Many fear the power that such an agency would inevitably acquire and the near impossibility of escaping from its reach: individuals would no longer be able to emigrate from an oppressive state to freedom in another state. To be even remotely acceptable to many, any global state would also have to be democratic in form and functioning. Intense debates continue, however, over the feasibility of maintaining democratic institutions for constituencies that are divided by diverse values and separated by disparate cultures. The possible need for effective and democratic global governance will not, in itself, ensure that the necessary conditions for such political institutions will come into being.[23]

If a democratic global state remains a problematical and remote possibility, then international management will have to continue to rest upon inter-state foundations, and domestic governance will have to be undertaken by state-like institutions. There may be intense debate about the identities of the state-like institutions that will survive or emerge – as in the case of autonomy debates in the regions of the United Kingdom or the advocacy of greater federalism by enthusiasts for an integrated Europe – but state-like institutions will be at the heart of effective governance.

The problem for the state, however, is that it is faced by substantial challenges. The reassertion of the state will therefore have to rest upon either the invention of new ways of achieving traditional objectives; the development of new patterns for the provision of desired public goods; or the adoption of measures designed to roll back some of the processes and developments that underlie the contemporary challenge to the state and its capabilities.

Inventing new ways of achieving traditional objectives is not a costly process for states and their populations. Dealing with the financial problems created by global financial integration and the mobility of transnational corporations and their leading employees has, for instance, prompted a shift from corporate taxation to increased levels of direct tax on the poorer members of the community, in combination with more reliance on indirect taxation, within many Advanced Industrial Countries. Both innovations have made the tax system of such countries increasingly regressive – that is imposing a proportionally greater overall tax burden upon the poorer members of society than upon the more wealthy (and more mobile).

Discussion of new patterns of public governance focuses upon the notion of 'multi-level' governance. The core idea here is that the issues generated in the contemporary world require management at different levels of political activity: some at the global level, some at regional level, some at traditional 'state' level', some at more local levels. Institutions of public governance would thus be developed at each level and endowed with powers and competencies appropriate to the effective management of the issues arising at each level. The evolving structure of governance within the European Union is often quoted as an example of such multi-level governance in practice.[24]

The continuing difficulty with the notion of multi-level governance, however, is its stability and durability in the face of major pressures and problems. If the legitimacy and robustness of institutions of public governance ultimately rest upon their capacity to provide a range of most valued public goods, then public interest and notions of legitimacy will tend to be focused on those institutions that actually deliver core public goods. The supply of security, public order and general economic well-being are likely to remain the core public goods for the foreseeable future and the public authorities that provide these goods are likely to attract the greatest popular loyalty and prove the most durable at times of difficulty. Multi-level governance may not, therefore, prove to be stable or to be durable in the face of pressing problems, if and when they arise; effective authority thus tending to concentrate upon agencies that are, or are seen to be, able to deliver core public.

The effective revival of traditional states or the consolidation of new, regional states, will, however, be possible if a number of contemporary developments are brought under the control of those state-like institutions. The freedom of action and manoeuvre of international financial actors, transnational corporations and global communications' agencies (including internet service providers) may have to be regulated in ways that some will find uncomfortable. There may, moreover, be a clash between the liberalising agendas of international agencies like the World Trade Organisation and the need of state-like authorities to reassert authority and control within an internationalised world economy. The paradox of such developments would be that the combined actions of transnationalising actors, as diverse as transnational motor car manufacturers and environmental protection movements – might prove to be such as to stimulate state-focused counter-actions that reduce the level of transnational action that is possible in tomorrow's world.

Conclusions

Viewing the world through the lens of fragmentation thus indicates the ways in which it may be difficult, or impossible, to solve the problems of fragmentation which have been enumerated in earlier chapters using conventional institutions and practices. Instead, it may be necessary to consider dramatically different approaches or paradigms.

Two realities?

Viewing international relations through the lens of fragmentation in a period of growing globalisation reveals two different and conflicting realities. On the one hand, there is the system of international relations that most analysts study and policy makers have to cope with in which the state remains by far the most important actor. On the other hand, many of today's problems are transnational in nature and cannot readily be addressed by states acting on their own and trying to maximise their national interest, especially as the Realists and other mainstream theorists define the term. In other words, the focus on fragmentation can take the analyses and, potentially, the stakes of international relations far beyond anything that has been considered thus far in this book.

Science fiction writers have long made much of stories about parallel universes that spark horrendous conflict on those rare occasions when they come into contact with each other. If analyses based on fragmentation are accurate, parallel universes are not a fantasy but a central component to today's international relations and, perhaps, the most important reason why so many problems are being encountered in solving many of the world's most vexing problems

The stakes are now higher than ever. The direst plausible predictions about environmental decay or an all-out nuclear war include the end of civilisation as we know it. Most of the other dangers faced today may not put humanity itself at risk, but overpopulation, the spread of AIDS, conventional wars fought over religious or ethnic issues, crime and terrorism can and often do exact a high, and potentially very high, human toll.

It is increasingly difficult to separate international from other issues. As was seen in the section on the internal workings of the state, the intellectual fire wall between IR and the rest of political science has been irrevocably breached. It is now necessary to consider not only domestic as well as international political sources but also economic, environmental, social and cultural factors.

It is now increasingly difficult, if not impossible, to tackle one international issue without addressing the entire range of problems. Rather like an onion, world affairs are now such that, on peeling away one layer (the environment) another is encountered (poverty in the less developed part of the world); peeling away that layer and yet another is encountered (the costs of militarisation and war). The overlapping nature of global problems was the main reason why the UN planners had to turn the 1992 Rio Summit into a session on the environment and development.

The world is changing at an unprecedented and accelerating rate. The pace of political, social, economic, cultural and technological change may not be raising the stakes of international relations in and of itself. However, there is little doubt that there is far more uncertainty to international relations as a result, which, in turn, makes everything more unpredictable, thus increasing the likelihood of the kinds of misperceptions described in the sections dealing with the internal workings of the state.

Global problems no longer appear to be amenable to traditional political solutions in which one side imposes its will on the other. The Gulf war, the most serious crisis of this decade so far, provides a single and compelling example. Iraq was forced out of Kuwait, but, that came at tremendous cost, and none of the other underlying problems which led to the war (e.g., instability in the region, Arab distrust of the West, the Iraqi regime itself) were resolved. That was made abundantly clear in the repeated unrest inside Iraq, the resistance of its government to the UN-imposed sanctions, the threats it continued to pose to its neighbours, and the two major military reactions by the United States and its allies in the years since the Gulf War.

Global problems thus seem to require some sort of cooperative, win–win solution. Cooperative solutions are required, because, by their very nature, no one nation or group or individual can solve any of these problems on its own. That is perhaps easiest to see with the environment, where, for instance, ending the destruction of the Amazonian rain forest seems to require joint action by the North and South through, for instance, debt-for-nature swaps, in which Developing Countries receive debt relief in exchange for promises to protect some aspect of their environments.

This list suggests there is what the clinical psychologists call a 'dissociation' between the two realities of international relations. On the one hand, problems continue to be addressed through a state-based system in what the former advisor to French President François Mitterrand and former head of the European Bank for Reconstruction and Development, Jacques Attali, calls the struggle for supremacy in which each side tries either to win or, at worst, to keep itself from losing.

However, most states may be losing their capacity to deal with most of the new issues that make up the agenda of international relations as the twentieth century draws to a close. Perhaps even more worrying is the fact that the politics of winners and losers is itself creating an ever more perilous situation. In economics, for example, the short-term losers are likely to be the peoples of the poorest countries in the third world and the long-term loser, could be the biosphere itself. As Jacques Attali put it '[i]f the market alone is relied upon to build whole societies, it will end up producing the principle revolutionaries of tomorrow who will rise in resentment against the wealthy inhabitants of the privileged centres of the world'.[25]

Lists of issues now facing humanity, thus lead some observers who focus on fragmentation to an even broader conclusion that the real problem is the way in which international relations have been analysed and conducted in general: an injunction that challenges the very foundations of the subject as it has been studied and taught traditionally. However, the uncertainties about the pattern of future developments and serious doubts about the viability of non-state forms of governance leave serious questions about whether alternatives to a state-centred world may not be far worse than a modified and enhanced system of states, with new inter-state institutions for coordination, collaboration and cooperative approaches to the many growing problems of mutual interest and concern.

Notes

1 Many of these empirical developments and some of their more important intellectual implications are discussed in: James N. Rosenau, *Turbulence in World Politics: A Theory of Change and Continuity* (Hemel Hempstead: Harvester/ Wheatsheaf, 1990).

2 See the discussion in R.J. Barry Jones, *The World Turned Upside Down?: Globalisation and the Future of the State* (Manchester: Manchester University

Press, 2000), pp. 176–85.

3 On which see: David Held, *Democracy and the Global Order: From the Modern State to Cosmopolitan Governance* (Cambridge: Polity Press, 1995); and B.B. Holden (ed.), *Global Democracy: Key Debates* (London: Routledge, 2000).

4 On the serious weaknesses of which see: R.J. Barry Jones, *The World Turned Upside Down?*, esp. chapter 8.

5 On early signs of which see: K.J. Holsti, *The Dividing Discipline* (London: Allen & Unwin, 1987).

6 For a further discussion of which see: Charles Hauss, *International Conflict Resolution* (London: Pinter, 2001).

7 Frances Cairncross, *The Death of Distance: How the Communications Revolution with Change our Lives* (London: Orion Business Books, 1997).

8 Martin Shaw, *Global Society and International Relations: Sociological Concepts and Political Perspectives* (Cambridge: Polity Press, 1994).

9 On which see: Ross H. Mclleod and Ross Garnaut, *East Asia in Crisis: From Being a Miracle to Needing One?* (London: Routledge, 1988); and R.J. Barry Jones, *The World Turned Upside Down?*, chapter 10.

10 For some of the dimensions of this see the contributions to: B. Hansen and B. Heurlin (eds), *The New World Order: Contrasting Theories* (Harmondsworth: Macmillan, 2000).

11 On which see the entry by Robert Looney on, 'Neo-liberalism' in R.J. Barry Jones (ed.), *The Routledge Encyclopaedia of International Political Economy* (London: Routledge, 2001).

12 On a form of which see: Paul Hirst, *Associative Democracy* (Cambridge: Polity Press, 1993).

13 On collective (and public) goods see: R.J. Barry Jones, *The World Turned Upside Down?*, chapter 7, esp. pp. 180–5.

14 On these points see the contributions by R.J. Barry Jones. 'Social science, globalisation and the problem of the state' and Michael Mann, 'Neither nation state nor globalism', *Environment and Planning A*, 28, 11 (November, 1996), 1948–53, 1960–4.

15 Particularly anarchists, see: George Woodcock, *Anarchism: A History of Libertarian Ideas and Movements* (Harmondsworth: Penguin books, 1963).

16 An issue considered in depth in, J. N. Rosenau and E.O. Czempiel (eds), *Governance without Government: Order and Change in World Politics* (Cambridge: Cambridge University Press, 1992).

17 See the discussion of multi-level governance at the international level in: Richard Bellamy and R.J. Barry Jones, 'Globalisation and Democracy: An Afterword', in B.B. Holden (ed.), *Global Democracy: Key Debates* (London: Routledge, 2000), pp. 202–16.

18 R.J. Barry Jones, *The World Turned Upside Down?*, esp. chapter 4; and also the discussions in M. Shaw (ed.), *Politics and Globalisation: Knowledge, Ethics and Agency* (London: Routledge, 1999).

19 For the classic review of transnational relations and transnational patterns of association see: R.O. Keohane and J.S. Nye (eds), *Transnational Relations and World Politics* (Cambridge, MA: Harvard University Press, 1971) (reprint of special edition of *International Organisation*, 25, 3 (Summer, 1971).

20 See the report in *The Economist*: 'Worries about Rio', 7 January 1996, pp. 22–3.

21 See R.P. Bellamy and R.J. Barry Jones, 'Globalisation and Democracy: An Afterword', pp. 202–16.

22 See, for example, the debates in the contributions to: S. Smith, K. Booth and M. Zalewski (eds), *International Theory: Positivism and Beyond* (Cambridge: Cambridge University Press, 1996).

23 See Bellamy and Jones, 'Globalisation and Democracy'.

24 Ibid.

25 Jacques Attali, *Winners and Losers in the Coming World Order* (trans. Leila Conner and Nathan Gardels) (New York: Times Books, 1991), p. 71.

Further reading

Clark, Ian, *Globalisation and Fragmentation: International Relations in the Twentieth Century* (Oxford: Oxford University Press, 1997). A historically well-informed discussion of contemporary globalisation.

Ferguson, Yale and R.J. Barry Jones (eds), *Political Space: The Frontiers of International Relations Theory* (New York: State University of New York, 2000). A collection of discussions of changing patterns of politics and governance.

Goldsmith, James, *The Trap* (London: Macmillan, 1994). An impassioned polemic against globalisation and further international economic liberalisation.

Greider, William, *One World, Ready or Not* (New York: Simon & Schuster and London: Allen Lane, Penguin Press, 1997). A popular account of globalisation.

Holden, B.B. (ed.), *Global Democracy: Key Debates* (London: Routledge, 2000). A collection of discussions of the prospects and problems of new global level forms of democratic governance.

Jones, R.J. Barry, *The World Turned Upside Dow?: Globalisation and the Future of the State* (Manchester: Manchester University Press, 2000). A wide-ranging discussion of the nature of globalisation and its possible effects upon the state and public governance.

Rosenau, J.N., *Turbulence in World Politics: A Theory of Change and Continuity* (Hemel Hempstead: Harverster/Wheatsheaf, 1990). An influential review of the contemorary world condition and the profound uncertainties created by recent developments.

Rosenau, J.N. and E.O. Czempiel (eds), *Governance without Government: Order and Change in World Politics* (Cambridge: Cambridge University Press, 1992). An interesting collection of papers on the complexities of governance in a globalised world.

Shaw, Martin Shaw, *Global Society and International Relations: Sociological Concepts and Political Perspectives* (Cambridge: Polity Press, 1994). A wide-ranging discussion of the possible advent of a new global society.

8 Conclusion

This selective review of some of the major approaches to international relations, past and present, has been intended to introduce students to some of the central ideas with which the subject has been studied during the twentieth century and some of the ideas (and developments) that will concern students in the twenty-first. Not every theory and approach has been considered in detail and not every methodological debate has been plumbed to its labyrinthine depths. However, it is to be hoped that something of value will have been gained by the student of contemporary international relations.

Traditional approaches to international relations were discussed in some detail, as a way of introducing students to ideas that have been important in the past – both as the basis of study and as guides to the conduct of world affairs – and that may well continue to be of some importance in future relations amongst groups of human beings who conceive themselves to be separate from one another in legal, if not always in all practical, respects. The sources of international conduct lying within the individual human being, the state and society within which most human beings continue to live, and then the international system itself, thus all command continued attention. Such 'traditional' perspectives seemed to be particularly well suited to the era of big power politics and the Cold War and will continue to have considerable resonance within tomorrow's world. However, many new developments in world affairs now appear to challenge the state-centred world, and associated analytical perspectives.

Three ultimately inter-related perspectives upon contemporary developments embrace much of the current uncertainty about how the world is evolving and how best it should be studied. Globalisation embraces many of the developments in the economic, technical, social and cultural arenas that underlie much of the contemporary dynamic. There are, however, considerable uncertainties about the character, extent and implication of globalisation. Such uncertainties underpin uncertainties about the pattern of future developments.

Increasing regionalisation offers one possible pattern of response to contemporary pressures and developments, particularly for beleaguered governments seeking to restore some measure of control over an apparently runaway world economy. However, regionalisation also raises substantial questions about the primacy of politics, economics or technology in the shaping of world developments and, hence, the durability of contemporary efforts to construct regional associations of states and economies.

Increased regionalisation itself might mark one form of fragmentation of the global political system. 'Fortresses' Europe and North America might be able to isolate themselves from many of the more turbulent developments elsewhere, maintaining only those lines of supply of resources that will continue to be essential to the economic well-being of these macro-regions of affluence. However, self-regarding regions might not be sustainable in the face of growing global turbulence. Fragmentation might, moreover, not be confined merely to division into macro-regions, but proceed further to undermine the stability of both of these regions and their constituent societies. The revival of myriad religious and ethnic divisions attests to the divisive possibilities that still abound within the contemporary world. Indeed, it remains a very real possibility that inter-cultural and inter-regional tensions within many AICs will, in the end, precipitate similar fragmentary tendencies as they have in so many LDCs and former Soviet Bloc societies during the last decades of the twentieth century.

Intellectual fragmentation has also marked the turn of the century/millennium. There is nothing new about such an intellectual kaleidoscope. Ideas and approaches tend to clarify and simplify at times of serious and pressing problems in the real world. While there are many very real problems confronting the world at the start of the twenty-first century, few of these have yet impacted upon the populations of the world's more affluent societies with the sharpness of the First World War, the communist revolution in Russia, the rise of Fascism and Nazism within Europe, the Second World War or the Cold War. Equally, the passing of the simplicities of the era of decolonisation have deprived many of the LDCs of the intellectual certainties with which they approached independence. The start of the twenty-first century is thus characterised by a kind of intellectual adolescence: a period of freedom to explore all manner of exciting ideas before the pressures of adult life compel greater caution and responsibility.

The future is, indeed, likely to confront humanity with many serious problems and choices, which will inevitably be reflected in the perspectives of students of international relations. Francis Fukuyama's vainglorious proclamation of the 'end of history' is now widely acknowledged to have been misplaced. Resource and environmental issues are likely to prove both pressing and potentially highly divisive during coming decades. The world economy also continues to encompass serious areas of potential instability and it remains an open question as to whether the ever-more complex mosaic of international organisations and regulative agencies will prove capable of dealing with serious crises in the future.[1] Moreover, the revival of ideological divisions and confrontations cannot be ruled out; indeed, violent ideologies have flourished precisely at times of economic difficulty. Moreover, notions of religious, ethnic, cultural or 'national' difference also continue to permeate much of humanity, waiting only upon adverse developments and/or the emergence of charismatic leaders to erupt into violent and aggressive expression.

More specifically, the world will continue to confront pressures on resources. Markets offer one apparently impersonal mechanism for the management of scarcity of resources, but those whose access is denied by lack of purchasing power tend to see this 'impersonal' mechanism in a rather more personal, and unfavourable, light. Moreover, some resources – like those of water in the Middle East – have been allocated as much through political control as by any purely economic process.

The working through of resource pressures will be a complex matter in the kind of world that we now inhabit. Resource rich LDCs can benefit from resource scarcities – as witnesses by some of the oil-exporting countries in the latter decades of the twentieth century – but even this advantage can be countered by increased vulnerability to pressure (and even invasion) by those who covet such resources – as in the case of Iraq's occupation of Kuwait in the early 1990s. More seriously, however, resource-poor LDCs are always badly affected by shortages of important natural resources, which inevitably translate themselves into higher prices.

AICs have often been affected by those resource shortages that translate themselves into higher prices. However, the financial burden has often been more manageable by the richer countries, which also have considerable capacities for technological innovation directed towards the development of substitutes for previously essential resources or access to new sources of such resources.

Similar (but not necessarily identical) asymmetries also characterize the creation, and experience, of the effects of environmental damage, such as global warming. Richer countries clearly have far greater economic resources with which to meet any adverse environmental developments than poorer countries. While an abundance of resources will not preserve rich countries from all damaging effects, it will enable them to provide measures of protection and/or compensation in all but the most severe of cases. Poorer countries, by contrast, are likely to be hapless victims of the most serious forms of environmental disruption, with consequential humanitarian disasters and/or massively increased migratory movements towards less-threatened territories.

Even without resource shortages and environmental disasters, it is by no means clear that the world has yet discovered a practical formula for ensuring both the general advance of prosperity and a reduction of the glaring, and often deepening, pattern of inequality that marked the late twentieth century. The problem is that, even if it were possible to avoid the actual reduction of income that has been experience by a number of African countries that have fallen prey to civil war and general strife, the continuation of marked disparities of economic well-being tends to breed deep dissatisfaction and resentment. Moreover, the spread of global communications and cultural products increases the visibility of those disparities of wealth and well-being that have long existed, but not always been so apparent to those at the bottom of the global heap. The received wisdom at the start of the twentieth century is that many of the aggressive impulses being expressed within the Middle East (and elsewhere) are not so much a function of religious or ethnic factors (Islamic 'fundamentalism' for example) but a product of the continued deprivation and lack of prospects of the populations within which such impulses are born.

Global inequalities do not, however, exhaust the dangers lurking within the developing global political economy. There remain considerable dangers that runaway globalisation will eventually plunge the world economy into crisis. The extent and speed of global economic and financial integration has been such as to increase, massively, the scale of international exchanges, transactions and financial flows. The result is a world economy that is more tightly interconnected and in which disruptions in one part (geographically or spectrally) can be transmitted more rapidly and with a greater impact than in the past. The stability of such a system is, therefore, increasingly dependent upon the effectiveness of self-regulating mechanisms (particularly market mechanisms) or, when they fail as they often do, upon the regulative capabilities of national and international agencies. The Asian financial crisis of 1997–8 demonstrated the nature and danger of such a failure of self-regulating mechanisms within a globalised financial and economic system and the difficulties encountered by governmental agencies, national and international, in seeking to restore confidence and stability. A future repetition of such a crisis cannot be ruled out and might well be more severe in its character and effects. The consequences of such an intensified international economic crisis might, in turn, be such as to destabilise democratic governance in many parts of the world and revive international divisions and tensions.

Whatever the detailed developments that confront the world, and its students, during coming decades, the overwhelming likelihood is that it will remain an interesting place (in the Chinese sense of identifying interesting times with disorder and disruption). The kinds of developments that will be of concern in the twenty-first century will need to be analysed with as many and as varied intellectual tools as can be mustered. The perspectives upon international relations that have been considered in this volume are some of the more prominent perspectives that will permit the trials and tribulations of the future to be brought under some form of intellectual control. Whether they will also be sufficient to bring such developments under practical control will be for history to judge.

Note

1 Francis Fukuyama, *The End of History and the Last Man* (London: Hamish Hamilton, 1992).

Index